BASQUE-AMERICANS AND A SEQUENTIAL THEORY
OF MIGRATION AND ADAPTATION

A Thesis

San Francisco State College

by

Grant Edwin McCall
II

1968

Reprinted in 1973 by

R AND E RESEARCH ASSOCIATES
4843 Mission Street, San Francisco 94112
18581 McFarland Avenue, Saratoga, California 95070

PUBLISHERS AND DISTRIBUTORS OF ETHNIC STUDIES

Editor: Adam S. Eterovich
Publisher: Robert D. Reed

LIBRARY OF CONGRESS CARD CATALOG NUMBER

72-85226

ISBN

0-88247-230-5

FOREWORD

The aim of this thesis is to explore the regularities and common patterns to be found in the related phenomena of acculturation, urbanization, and immigration and to place Basques living in the United States within the context of this data.

To accomplish the first part, the general literature was reviewed. My thanks must be to Dr. John Adair for his assistance in directing me to this body of data. I would also like to thank him for his understanding and encouragement during the course of my relationship with him for the past two years at San Francisco State College. The second part of my work is drawn from three years' "part-time" field work among Basques living in the United States and Mexico City. The material is the result of participant-observation at various Basque functions in California, Nevada, Idaho, and New York City, as well as formal open ended interviews with members of these communities conducted primarily during my visits to their communities over three summers.

Bibliographic references on Basques in this country were gathered also over this three-year period and represent the assistance of both individual Basques and formal institutions, such as the Bancroft Library, the Library of the Los Angeles County Museum of Natural History, the California State Library, the Harney County Library, and the Idaho State Historical Society Library. A special note of thanks must be given to Mrs. Sheila N. McHugh who is herself responsible for having found a number of the Basque references cited in this work and whose conscientious attention to detail has more than once uncovered data I might otherwise have missed.

To facilitate the work of future researchers, I have listed those works related to Basques in the United States in a separate bibliography which follows the general bibliography. References cited in the thesis may refer to either of these bibliographies since the Basque material is not duplicated in the general bibliography.

My thanks must also be given to Dr. William Douglass of the Basque Studies Program of the University of Nevada at Reno for the facilities and consultation with which he has provided me. I feel that his future work and the work of the Institute which he heads, will prove to be of great value to Basque studies in particular and to the larger field of anthropology in general.

Dr. David Ames, in his capacity as a teacher and as a member of my thesis committee, has also provided valuable suggestions and comments. Dr. Robert T. Anderson, Department of Anthropology, Mills College, graciously offered his time to my efforts, including some valuable comments on voluntary associations. Thanks is also due to Mrs. Alice Parker who typed the manuscript.

Unfortunately, it is not possible to list the names of all the persons who have given of their time and energy to my research, but I would like to mention those who were especially helpful: Abel Bolamburu, Frederic Fuldain, Jean Leon Irribaren, Mr. and Mrs. Pierre Arrabit, and Odette Etcheverry, of San Francisco; Mrs. Florence Camino, of Buffalo, Wyoming; Mr. Jean Urruty, of Grand Junction, Colorado; Albert Erquiaga, Mrs. Rufino Hormachea, Mr. and Mrs. Julian Lachiando, of Boise, Idaho; Mr. and Mrs. Joe Eiguren, of Homedale, Idaho; Father Joseph K. Mallea, Antonio Uriarte, and Sr. Cipriano Larrañaga, the Delegate of the Basque Government in Exile to the United States, of New York City; Mr. Joe Uberuaga, Sr. Martin Garcia-Urtiaga, Sr. Antonio Ruiz de Azua de Zaballeta, of Mexico City; Father J. Challet,

Mr. Rafael Spring and his late wife Mary, of Fresno, California; Mr. and Mrs. Mike Fondi, of Ely, Nevada; Jean Lekumberry, of Gardnerville-Minden, Nevada; Louis Uriarte, of Elko, Nevada; and V. J. "Vyts" Beliajus, editor and publisher of Viltis magazine.

While I acknowledge the assistance and advice of those persons mentioned above, it is I, of course, who must take the blame for any blunders or mistakes.

May 8, 1968

TABLE OF CONTENTS

INTRODUCTION

Important in the study of anthropology is an understanding and appreciation of cultural dynamics. Processes of cultural change highlight aspects of a given culture or contribute to considerations of the nature of culture in a cross cultural view)Spiro, 1249). Halpern, in describing his research on the urbanization of peasants in Yugoslavia carried considerations of understanding change farther when he states that, "An anthropology of the future must be able to conceptualize drastic [emphasis mine] change without question (Halpern, n.d.: 10)."

But, drastic change, while it may be important to the masses of people undergoing it today, is but one facet of culture change in general.

Ralph Beals, in his presidential address to the American Anthropological Association, has noted that "within the framework subsumed by the concepts of urbanization and acculturation, we are dealing with processes which, if not identical, at least form a related continuity of social phenomena (Beals, 6)." In this address, he calls for anthropologists to work more closely with their sociology colleagues, as well as other disciplines, in order that such combined and multi-disciplinary research "will ultimately lead to the development of a common body of concepts and generalizations applicable to an everwidening body of phenomena (6). Cross-cultural studies of urbanization and urbanism, outside of a Western context, are also recommended as useful for finding regularities (Beals, 6).

To the similarities between urbanization and acculturation, I would like to add that many features of immigration, as I hope to point out below, are comparable. In fact, I would agree with Clifford Barnett's comments that the processes involved in migration may be seen as forms of the larger problem of "adult socialization (Barnett, 84)." I would prefer to view that part of adult socialization concerned with migration and adaptation.

Of the three processes, immigration is the only one in which movement is a constant feature. To be an immigrant, one must have moved from one locale to another. That is simple enough. For my purposes, it will be necessary that I distinguish between immigrant acculturation and urbanization and what I would like to call in situ acculturation and urbanization (Anderson and Anderson, 159). The latter category, of course, means that a person is subjected to acculturation or urbanization in his home setting. While there may be some functional corrolates for the immigrant and in situ categories of these phenomena, I would prefer not to deal with them at this time, but, rather to concentrate on their "immigrant" forms.

Thus, in all of the cases I intend to discuss, it is a group of immigrants in an unfamiliar context who are the actors. They have moved from their home setting into a "foreign" setting.

This does not mean that I am only going to consider immigrants moving from one country to another. Immigrants who move from rural to urban areas or rural to rural areas are also accounted for in the examination below.

By looking at urbanization, acculturation, and immigration, I have been able to derive some postulates regarding regularities of process for these phenomena. Before defining further my intentions, it is necessary to settle upon some working definitions of some of the concepts with which I shall be working.

1

Immigrant I define as any actor who moves from his home area to another settlement area for the purpose of living and working. I exclude from this migratory
workers since they are very special types in themselves. It is assumed that immigrants will settle within a given foreign context, though they may move around
within it. Thus, a family or individual might move to a series of apartments in
a given city, but not leave the city and still be considered as immigrants. Also,
a certain assumption is made that an immigrant is part of a larger immigration
from his home area to a given destination. The processes involved in my discussion are primarily those of a group nature and, except for some probable psychological corrolates, it is not likely that they would have much applicability to
the migration of a lone individual who lacked any supportive group.

I have chosen the term "immigrant" over one often used by other investigators,
"migrant," because "immigrant" implies purpose in movement, where "migrant" could
easily be seen as one who may move for the sake of moving without explicit purpose.
Certainly, my definition makes it clear that what I am talking about is a purpose-
ful movement from one context to another. The dilemma of the immigrant is thus:

> When a member of one culture migrates to another culture, he learns
> a system in which he has a place that affords him rights and obli-
> gations, and in which he has learned ways of fulfilling his obliga-
> tions and getting what is due him, and also has leanred what he is
> to expect. In order to survive in the new environment, the migrant
> [read immigrant] must build new relationships with new people and
> institutions (Kemnitzer, 1964:3).

Acculturation may be seen as "cultural transmission in process" (emphasis his,
Herskovits, 170). By one index, the term "acculturation" did not appear in the
anthropological literature until 1929 (Redfield) and then only by inference (Editor,
972).

Acculturation has also been seen as "culture change that is initiated by the
conjunction of two or more autonomous cultural systems (Social Science Research
Council, 974)." In another view of the process, Herskovits has detailed the various
forms of contact by which acculturation may occur:

> The first kind of situation to be envisaged is where elements of
> culture are forced on a people, or where acceptance is voluntary.
> The second situation is where no social or political inequality
> exists between groups. In the third situation, three alterna-
> tives are presented - that is, where there is political dominance
> but not social; where dominance is both political and social; and
> where social superiority of one group over another is recognized,
> without there being political dominance (Herskovits, 176-177).

Other terms, such as "transculturation" (Herskovits, 173) have been proposed
to replace acculturation in order that the dynamic process of transition from one
culture to another be made more explicit.[1] Acculturation may obviously be brought
into a discussion of urbanization and immigration if the immigrant (using my definition) is from another country than the one he is settling in. This is probably
recognized by most anthropologists under these circumstances. But, in the literature I have examined I am often talking about rural to urban migration within the
same culture. I would submit that in terms of the immigrant's view, a move from a
village to a city is a change in culture. Since Kroeber and Kluckhohn's work on

the concept of culture in anthropology, it has become clear, I feel, that culture is probably best seen as a clustering of traits. Contiguous cultures are related and even some formulas have been worked out for cross-cultural work to lesson the errors caused by similarities between cultures because of proximity (Murdock). Thus, a small village may be said to have a different culture than a large city, even if, politically, they are considered part of the same "culture."[2] Thus, the move from a peasant village in Yugoslavia to Belgrade (Halpern, n.d.) or a Kentucky village to southern Ohio (Brown, Schwarzeller, and Mangalam), represents just as great a change (expecially in terms of the processes I intend to delineate) as a Japanese moving to Chicago (Caudill and DeVos).

The final goal of acculturation, urbanization, or immigration, in their traditional meanings, is usually assimilation or, better said, adaptation.[3] While it is true that adaptation does not necessarily follow acculturation (Spiro, 1244) it is usually seen as the desired goal. Thus, in my examination, "assimilation" will be seen in terms of successful adaptation. By successful adaptation, I mean acquiescence to or ability to get along with the norms of the dominant culture. This is mainly seen in terms of overt, observable behavior and, often, in terms of economic behavior. Only rarely has the state of the immigrant and the desirability of such adaptation been questioned (Barnett, 87). In the context of the United States, adaptation usually means conformity to so-called middle class norms of occupational behavior and life style.

Acculturation and adaptation are very closely related. For most studies, I think it would be accurate to say that acculturation is generally the task of the immigrant group, while allowing adaptation is most often the prerogative of the "host" or receiving dominant group. So, in the American setting, a person may take an "approved" job, marry, and conduct his life in the perceived style of those around him but might not be fully accepted, and therefore unable to completely adapt because of something, say, such as visible "racial" markers. Caudill and DeVos have noted, at least, for the American context, how racial markers may frustrate the acculturative efforts of immigrants. Mestizos with "Indian characteristics" in Mexico appear to often have this problem, along with Koreans in Japan (DeVos and Wagatsuma), aborigines in Australia (Jones), or Lebanese in East Africa (Creet).

As a side note, I might mention that the processes of immigration, urbanization, and acculturation are often seen as destructive both to the "cultures" involved and to the individuals attempting the adaptation (Cowgill). Though Chance is here describing acculturation, many of the same things have been said about immigration and urbanization as destructive forces:

> Following initial contact, conflict in roles and values, drastic
> ecological and demographic shifts, changing levels of aspiration,
> and use of coercion and force by the dominant group to attain its
> objectives, are but a few of the many conditions predisposing to
> ... disorganization (Change, 372).

I do not intend, in my examination, to propose a harmonius "Melting Pot" idea of these processes, as mainly expressed in the writings of some Americans in the nineteenth century (Glazer and Moynihan).[4] But, I also do not want to give the impression that adaptation as an end goal, means that the immigrant gives up all of his culture to take on the culture of his new environment. As the Social Science Research Council Summer Seminar on Acculturation[5] asserted:

> Acculturation [or urbanization] is ... neither a passive nor a color-
> less absorption. It is a culture-producing as well as a culture-
> receiving process. Acculturation particularly where not forced is
> essentially creative (Social Science Council, 985).

The same may be said for urbanization (Glazer and Moynihan).

What I intend to do in this paper is to formulate a series of postulates for tracing a sequential theory of migration and adaptation.[6] Literature on accultura-tion, immigration, and urbanization will be utilized in constructing these postu-lates because of the similarity in process between these phenomena. The articles used in my study represent a broad cross-section of areas throughout the world, but is not intended to be exhaustive or representative. Rather, I would hope to show that similarities do exist and are worthy of being tested in areas other than those I have described.

The literature employed in my examination in part one includes data on Mexico City (Lewis), Kentucky Highlands (Brown, Schwarzeller, and Mangalam), Yugoslav Peasants (Halpern, n.d., Halpern, 1964), Navajo in Denver, Colorado (Graves, 1965), Amerindians in San Francisco (Hirabayashi and Willard, Ablon, Swett, Kemnitzer, 1964), Greek peasants in Athens (Friedl), Spanish immigrants in Mexico City and Cuba (Kenny, 1961b, Kenny, 1962), Negroes, Puerto Ricans, Jews, Italians, and Irish in New York City (Glazer and Moynihan), Eskimos on Barter Island (Chance), Poles in American (Schermerhorn), Japanese in Kona, Hawaii (Embre), Ukrainians in France (Anderson and Anderson), Egyptian peasants in Cairo (Ubu-Lughod), Japanese in Chicago (Caudill and DeVos), the Toba Batak urban migration in North Sumatra (Bruner, 1961), Mandan Hidatsa in Lone Hill (Bruner, 1956), Peteneros in Flores, Guatemala (Reina), Italians in Chicago (Vecoli), Lebanese in West Africa (Creet), Greeks in the United States (Saloutos, 1964), Swedes in the United States (Lindberg), and Italians in Norristown, United States (Ianni).[7]

Not all of the postulates I have derived below are to be found represented in each of the sources cited above, though this is sometimes the case. The writers represented above come from a variety of disciplines, including history, psychology, anthropology, economics, political science and their interests and level of analysis vary, so that I have not attempted to compare the data from these cases. Rather, I see this body of data on similar phenomena as a pool of common experiences and processes from which I may draw regularities of process.

Part II will be the testing ground. For my postulates and the sequence in which they appear to fall, I shall use data from my research among Basque-Americans.

I would urge other students of migration and adaptation to apply my thoughts to cases with which they have comprehensive data and to thus test their possible validity in a larger context than I have been able to do here. Therefore, I would say as did Steward, that "criticisms of this paper which concern facts alone and which fail to offer better formulations are of no interest (Steward, 25)."

PART I

POSTULATES FOR TRACING A SEQUENTIAL THEORY
OF MIGRATION AND ADAPTATION

CHAPTER I

THE ROLE OF THE CULTURE OF THE IMMIGRANT

The home culture of the immigrant will assist or hinder migration and adaptation. Hirabayashi, in his study of American Indian settlements in the San Francisco Bay Area has pointed out that "The greater the compatibility of values between the native and the urban culture, the greater the ease of adjustment (Hirabayashi and Willard, 43)."

In discussing urbanization, Bruner feels that two major factors are responsible for the degrees and type of urbanization of any given group, "the nature of the native culture and the conditions of urbanization (Bruner, 1961:519)."

This sort of preparation for the immigrant, whether it be intentional training or merely the unconscious influence of the nature of the immigrant's culture, may work to assist or hinder the immigrant in his attempts at adapting to new new environment.[8]

The Social Science Research Council Summer Seminar on Acculturation chose to look at the immigrants' culture in terms of it being "a flexible vs. a rigid system (975)." They postulated that a flexible system in a given culture will give the immigrant a greater variety of methods by which he may fulfill his roles, thus allowing him greater agility in the manner he chooses to adopt in his new environment. They would even advance their speculations to such an extent as to say that an "analysis of the compatibility of systemic patterns yields useful generalizations on the typological level and provides a basis for predicting [emphasis mine] acculturative influences (Social Science Research Council, 983)."

Cohen, as well as others, has pointed out the importance of family structure and how this might affect an immigrant's ability to work within a new environment. An emphasis on the nuclear family leads to having one adult male (the father) as a figure with which to identify. This, in turn, helps a person to have more self-confidence and, in turn, to succeed (Cohen, 1966:420). With the extended family, Cohen feels, a male, usually the one responsible for the support of a family, has a number of father images with which to identify and is thus confused and less self-reliant, a quality which Cohen feels is necessary for successful migration (Cohen, 1966:420).

Caudill and DeVos discuss the success of the Japanese in Chicago and note that a compatibility of values is an important function of this success:

> Traditionally, Japanese culture, social structuring values, and religion are thought of as alien to those of America. Moreover, the Issei [immigrant Japanese] has a background of rural, peasant, subsistence farming, and came to the United States with only temporary settlement in mind. Most important of all, the Japanese are a racially visible group to race-conscious Americans [yet, by 1947, Nissei, second-generation Japanese], almost as a group, held white collar and skilled jobs within the general employment of the city (Caudill and DeVos, 1103).

In spite of these possible differences in the backgrounds of the Japanese and the "general American" cultures,

> There seems to be a significant compatibility (by no means identity) between the value systems found in the culture of Japan and the value system found in American Middle Class culture. This compatibility of values gives rise to a similarity in the psychological adaptive mechanisms in the two societies as they go about the business of living (Caudill and DeVos, 1107).

I am not saying, and neither are Caudill and DeVos, that exact congruence of systems of values is necessary to success. It is rather that they are compatible with each other and do not oppose or conflict with each other. For the Japanese, overt behavior, though generated by possibly different mechanisms, is compatible with the general American norm expectations.

> The Japanese and American middle class cultures share the values of politeness, respect for authority and parental wishes, duty to community, diligence, cleanliness and neatness, emphasis on personal achievement of long-range goals, importance of keeping up appearances, and others. [Also,] both Japanese and middle class Americans characteristically utilize the adaptive mechanism of being highly sensitive to cues coming from the external world as to how they should act, and that they also adapt themselves to many situations by supression of their real emotional feelings, particularly desires for physical aggressiveness (Caudill and DeVos, 1107).

For Spanish immigrants in Cuba, Kenny notes the importance of their background to their success on the island (Kenny, 1961b:86). A fuller examination of this background is to be found in his sketch of Spanish rural life (Kenny, 1961a).

Anderson and Anderson, in their report on Ukrainians in France note how the formation of voluntary associations was instrumental to their success in their environment and how a form of this institution had its origin in their home environment. [9]

Japanese settling in Kona, Hawaii also exhibited adaptive behavior based upon their home background (Embre) as did Poles in America (Schermerhorn), Italians in Chicago (Vecoli), Syrians in West Africa (Creet), Greeks in the United States (Saloutos, 1964), Swedes in the United States (Lindberg), and Japanese in Utah (Iga). The general tendency of success being related to cultural predisposing factors is surveyed by Bernard C. Rosen for a number of immigrant groups in the United States.

Glazer and Moynihan, in their examination of five immigrant groups in New York City, note cultural factors for all of their groups, except one - the American Negro. The section on the American Negro, written most probably by Moynihan, denies that blacks have any culture of their own: "The Negro is only an American and nothing else. He has no values to guard and protect (Glazer and Moynihan, 53)." Since they do so well in relating cultural factors to immigrant behavior for their other groups, I only point out this apparent discrepancy in passing. Much work in recent years has been done on the existence of culture for the American Negro (Horton).

Of particular interest in their work is an examination of Italian adaptation in New York City as being related to their family structure. They note that a type of "amoral familism" (Glazer and Moynihan, 195) has allowed the Italian in America to live in otherwise unsupportive environments in American cities and to be able to coexist with varied elements. For the family, whatever does not directly threaten the personal family life is not relevant for consideration or concern. Who lives next door and what he does is not directly of concern to the Italian family and they, therefore, do not become involved with it.

Numerous studies have also been done of American Indian adaption to American life. Consistently, the background of a given tribe has proven to be of tremendous influence upon the immigrants adaptive behavior. Thus, Indians who come to the city with a history of acculturative influences, consistently are able to adapt better (Martin). Swett has also pointed to differential reservation influences as they affect urban adaption. The presence of white models in the family of an Indian and the acculturative influence this exerts would seem to show a strong corrolation between primary group experiences and a tendency to adapt well (Bruner, 1956).

I have mentioned above that I would not deal much with the problem of adaption of a non-immigrant nature and that my primary concern would be with migration and adaptive behavior. I would like to make brief reference to one case of non-immigrant adaptive behavior, since it so well illustrates the influence of home culture on the immigrant. An example of such an examination of cultural factors is drawn from material on Barter Island Eskimos:

> While numerous factors were involved in this positive adjustment to rapid change, six appeared to be paramount: First, the Barter Island Eskimos have a predisposition to change already built into their sociological system in that a greater value was placed on adaptatility than on conformity; second, they voluntarily chose to change large segments of their social and cultural life to fit a Western model; third, the majority of the newly defined goals associated with these changes was capable of realization including economic affluence and positive interethnic relations; fourth, the community members participated in the changes together as a group, thereby circumventing the problem of inter-generational factionalism so frequently found in situations of acculturation; fifth, most of the major alternations of previous cultural patterns occurred together in such a manner as to preserve a total cultural balance; and sixth, the people were able to control their own internal village affairs without outside coercion (Chance, 373).

Such examinations of immigrant groups, in terms of their backgrounds, will lend greater validity and understandability to processes of adaption. Caudill and DeVos feel that achievement motivation is central to a drive for adaptive behavior and present a strong case for it with their Japanese-American material. While they stress the cultural background, as I do in this paper, they also wish to note the interplay between individually determined orientations and culturally determined orientations and note,

> the need for systematic investigation and interrelation of: (a) overt and underlying culture patterns, (b) individual psychodynamic

factors, (c) the structure and emotional atmosphere of crucial small group interactive settings in the home, on the job and recreation (Caudill and DeVos, 1123).

Unfortunately, my own work does not allow me the thoroughness of Caudill and DeVos, but I agree with their intentions and the usefulness of their suggestions.

CHAPTER II

THE ROLE OF THE DEGREE OF PRESSURE TO SUCCEED

The degree of the pressure to succeed exerted upon the immigrant to succeed is instrumental in the earnestness with which he applies himself to adaptation.

This chapter is very closely connected with the previous one on cultural factors. The previous chapter discussed the predisposing influences (Creet) of culture on the immigrant, while this examination seeks to show the adaptational aspect of these cultural factors. I will show that different groups see immigration in different terms and that while some allow their émigrés to return without necessarily being successful, others only allow a return, and then provisional, only if success has been achieved. For some groups, then, I will show, that the individual is almost "trapped" into adaptive behavior so as to gain favor with his home culture. I would speculate that such influences would be especially found among immigrants of societies with strong feelings of guilt and shame (Peristiany).

Kenny, in his discussion of Spaniards in Cuba (principally Galicians and Asturians), notes:

> The act of immigration does not automatically confer prestige; on the contrary, the New World immigrant is usually referred to, somewhat scornfully, as an indiano by his villagers and on his visits or return to the village he must often strive to reintegrate himself (Kenny, 1961b:91).

Even though the immigrant may see himself somewhat less than welcome in the home village, it is quite clear that approbation from his fellow home villagers is important to him, since Kenny notes that the New World Spaniard will often send money back to the village, to family or for public monuments, in order to gain prestige--to show that he has made it in the New World (Kenny, 1961b:91; Pitt-Rivers, 24). Kenny makes it clear that émigrés who have not made it are not welcome back in a village already unable to adequately support its resident population.

The Japanese-Americans in Caudill and DeVos' study also have a strong desire to succeed and feel that it is a "duty to one's parents, and [fulfills a] ... need to be of benefit to society (Caudill and DeVos, 1116).

Glazer and Moynihan have also made a point that pressure to succeed may not be a factor in adaptation if there is a conflict in the definitions of "success" between the immigrant's culture and the culture within which he is trying to make his way. Thus, the Italian-American is raised with an interest in "becoming," with little concern for future goals or expectations (Glazer and Moynihan, 198). So, little emphasis has been placed upon education, except as practical training for employment. In the Italian-American family, the "bad" son or daughter is the one who wants to prolong his schooling past an age when he might seek employment and bring money into the family (Glazer and Moynihan, 199). Thus, Italian-Americans, when they did go to college, went in heavily for such fields as engineering and were little involved with pedagogy or the professions (Glazer and Moynihan, 199). "Education," he concludes, "was seen as a means of preparing for a profession (Glazer and Moynihan, 202).

Glazer and Moynihan feel that American Catholics for the most part exhibit relatively little respect for social and occupational mobility, especially in the case of the Irish in America. They point to what they term "a general Catholic Failure" [their capitalization] in providing stimulus for achievement and success (Glazer and Moynihan, 358).

In the field of the exploration of factors relating to entrepreneurial activity (which I see as a striving for success), it is noted:

> that motivational disposition developed early in life define capaci-
> ties for satisfaction and interest in certain kinds of activity for
> which opportunity arises later in life (Atkinson, 109).

A strong need for achievement and association, engendered by an immigrant's culture has been seen as contributing to a cognitive orientation consistent with entrepreneurial activity (Atkinson, 109) and pressure upon the individual to succeed.

Greeks, in their early migrations to the United States in the beginning of the nineteenth century, on the other hand, felt no pressure to succeed and often did not. No substantial rewards awaited the successful retournee to Greece and their level of achievement was low because of this (Saloutos, 1964:44-70).

Entrepreneurial activity need not always be individual oriented and Lebanese in West Africa exhibit what has been termed a "corporate entrepreneurship," in which individual entrepreneurs appear to strive for success in terms of bettering the common lot of the Lebanese enclave rather than being concerned with individual goals (Creet, 39). Also, too, in Creet's example, Lebanese who are successful will often make this success known by sending money and costly gifts to persons in the home country.

Shepperson has noted how nineteenth century working class English coming to the United States often did not feel a pressure to succeed and indeed felt that if they should not do well in America, they could easily and honorably return to England (Shepperson, 179). A similar situation existed for Greeks and at one point immigration to the United States was exceeded by emigration bound for the home country! (Saloutos, 1965:199).

A similar situation exists for Kentucky mountaineers moving to Ohio. The investigators used LePlay's famillie-souche or "stem family," to show how immigrants were forced to emigrate as part of their life cycle, but that should they fail to be able to adapt well to their urban environment, they would be protected by their family and given a place to live all the same (Brown, Schwarzweller, and Mangalam, 67). Pressure to succeed was relatively lacking here as was successful adaptation.

In discussing peasant urban migration in general (without specifying any area), Potter notes how family ties will generally be maintained by the migrating peasant upon his first entry into the new environment and that "only after success are family ties generally broken (Potter, 379)." It would seem that relatively little immediacy would be placed upon immigrants having the option of returning and the above cases appear to bear this supposition out. This is the case for Yugoslav peasants (Halpern, n.d. and Halpern, 1964).

There are some groups of persons who practice a system of absolute inheritance of the family's properties and goods with the expectation that those non-inheriting

11

family members will leave the homestead and, possibly, the country. Such a system has the effect of forcing migration.

Lindberg notes the custom in Sweden of keeping the family gård (the farm and its lands) intact by leaving it to only one heir. The heir is chosen by the ruling member of the household and, in some areas in Sweden, this accounted for a good deal of emigration to the United States in the nineteenth and early twentieth centuries (Lindberg).

For Spaniards from many provinces of Spain, "Minifundia and systems of primogeniture seem to have created perverse economic conditions whereby migration [is] almost a necessity (Kenny, 1962:171)." These persons, forced to leave their homes, appear to be driven to success:

> Matured and skilled yet highly adaptable, and possessed of a desperate desire to make good which lent them boundless energy, they appeared to have overcome a number of obstacles not the least of which was ... opposition ... from certain Mexican groups (Kenny, 1962:176).

The Spanish immigrant was forced to leave his homeland and was driven to succeed so that he could fulfill his self-image of "the classic Indiano who expects to return in triumph to his native village, his pockets bulging with money (Kenny, 1962:177)."

Embree notes the influence of strict primogeniture on the emigration of rural Japanese to Hawaii and the feelings of necessity this creates upon the immigrant in his new environment (Embree, 403).

More on the order of the Swedish method of transferring goods, was that of the Poles. Strict primogeniture was not used, but absolute inheritance of property was and, I feel many of the same pressures put upon victims of strict primogeniture (with some important exceptions to be discussed in Part II) come into play. So,

> the father retired when one of his sons was better able to manage the homestead than he was; the favorite child took over the management of the farm--in central Poland, the eldest son, in the southern mountain areas the youngest son, and in some cases the one with the strongest personal qualities (Schmermerhorn, 410).

Even of course, when strong pressure to succeed is exerted, it does not mean that consistent success will be achieved. I merely mean to say that the chances of success are better if there is pressure to succeed. Why one person succeeds and another does not may be largely a matter of individual orientation (Caudill and DeVos) and might not be necessarily related to cultural pressures to do so.

Some cases report what happens when pressure to succeed is greater than the level of success the immigrant believes himself to have. Chance's Eskimo example notes that "the highest emotional disturbance scores [his emphasis] are found in those groups which show higher Western identification rank than contact rank (Chance, 381)." A similar finding is expressed in a study of drinking practices as a symptom of retreatism in a mixed Anglo, Spanish-American and Indian community in the Southwest (Graves, 1967:310-311). Sometimes, when pressure to succeed clashes with inhibitors to success exerted upon the immigrant, the ultimate form of human protest may occur--suicide (Maris).

12

It has also been noted that the American Indian has been often poorly prepared for an entry into the modern life of the United States and this may contribute to his often low level of success (Brophy).

CHAPTER III

THE ROLE OF KIN AND HOME-BASED ASSOCIATIVE TIES

There is a tendency for immigration to proceed along kin or other home-based associative ties.

In looking at immigration in general, Peterson has noted that:

> Once it is well begun, the growth of such a movement is semi-
> automatic; so long as there are people to emigrate, the principle
> cause of emigration is prior emigration (Peterson, 263).

What the first immigrants in a given area do and what their motives for coming are is probably due to the interplay of certain so-called "push-pull" factors (Bowers). The reasons why the immigrants who follow these pioneers appear to have a great deal to do with kinship or other home-based associative ties.

Kentucky Mountain migrants tend to follow kinship ties and have done so since 1942 (Brown, Schwarzweller and Mangalam, 1963:48).

Peasant immigrants to Cairo, Egypt also follow this kinship pattern. A "fairly typical pattern of initial settlement" for Egyptian immigrants is one which I feel also describes the initial phase of immigration in general for nearly all immigrant groups:

> The typical migrant ... is a young man whose first contact in the city
> is often with a friend or a relative from his original village, with
> whom he may even spend the first few nights. Later, more permanent
> lodgings are found, usually within the same neighborhood (Abu-Lughod,
> 388).

To show the prevalence of this pattern of migration, cross-culturally, a number of bibliographic works giving data on India, Asia, the Far East and Africa South of the Sahara may be cited (Abu-Lughod, 388).

Spanish expatriates in Mexico City exhibit differences between the general im-migrant and the exile from the Spanish Civil War. Though a difference exists in the nature of their migrations, I would tend, on the basis of data I have for Basques in Mexico City, to disagree with his distinction that:

> All groups except those exiled by the Civil War participated in the
> form of chain-migration whereby through kin, locality, ideological,
> or associational links of the patronage kind they were led directly
> to certain areas in Mexico and, often, into certain occupations
> (Kenny, 1962:170).

Greek peasants send their young men and women to Athens for different reasons for each sex. Males go to seek employment or education, while females are largely sent for the purpose of marriage and rarely for employment (Friedl, 57). Often a family will send a family member, even if only temporarily, "so that then there will be relatives there [in the city] for the other children to go to (Friedl, 61)." There is a great deal of reluctance to send young people to an urban setting without first having the kin ties for security and assistance in settlement. A similar situation and sequence appears also to exist for most Yugoslav peasant urban migrations (Halpern, n.d.:31).

American Indians moving into American cities are not always able to find ties of kinship, so they often seek locales to which other persons from their reservation or tribe have traveled previously (Kemnitzer, 1964; Ablon, 397). Peasant migration in North Sumatra also is found to largely follow kin ties (Bruner, 1961: 509).

A somewhat bizarre explanation of why groups tend to emigrate to areas already settled by members of their own family or home group was offered by an early "anatomist-turned-anthropologist, Dr. Robert Knox," in his book, The Races of Man published in 1850 (Hutchinson, 50). It was this researcher's opinion that if the "blood" of a migrated population was not "kept-up" in strength by the infusion of "new blood" from the home country, then the transplanted stock would soon wither and die (Hutchinson, 56). In his theory, he had some grave doubts, for example, that the "Caucasion race" could continue to survive in the New World without a constant renewing of their "race" by the arrival of new persons. He theorized that if Englishmen should ever stop emigrating to the New World, then English immigrants of previous times and their descendants would soon die. He appealed to Englishmen of his time to follow their ancestors for these reasons (Hutchinson, 57).

Other examples of the influence of kin or home-associative ties may be found in the literature on Japanese in Hawaii (Embre, 400), Swedes in the United States (Lindberg), Lebanese in West Africa (Creet), Italians in Chicago and New York City (Vecoli, Glazer and Moynihan), and, to some extent, for Japanese in Utah (Iga). Surveys of immigrant groups in general in Australia reveal similar patterns (Jones) as do surveys for immigrants in the United States (Handlin and Handlin, 1956).

American Indians in Western cities are often relocated with government assistance and have a choice of cities. Their choices are often directed by the existence of others of their tribe or clan living in a given area (Graves, 1965).

CHAPTER IV

THE ROLE OF THE TOKORO-MON

Fictive kin ties will be formed based upon locality in the absence of kin ties. Most immigrant groups find themselves migrating more along the lines of home-based associative ties and it is "only rarely ... [that] an immigrant finds himself near a member of his larger kinship group (Anderson and Anderson, 163)."

Thus, the immigrant was forced to seek out new relationships based upon non-blood kin ties. It has been noted for many groups that "the structure of those new relationships is, as a rule, based on the pattern of the old network of relationships as they existed in the original social situation (Embre, 400). The immigrant, when faced with a choice of whether to associate initially with the unfamiliar natives of his new region or members of his own group, usually chooses the old group to depend upon.[10] Among the general group, there was a marked preference for choosing persons from the same village or province--a "same-place-man," or Tokoro-mon. The term is taken from a study of Japanese in Kona, Hawaii. "Kinship" or a special relationship is recognized and ritualized on the basis of coming from the "same place (Embre, 406)." The tendency and degree for ritualizing actual "kin" relations probably varies from group to group, but most groups appear to recognize someone from their own "home area" as being special, at least for the first generation, after which such bases for association tend to lose their strength (Embre, 407).

Often, rather than a specific village, a region will be recognized as the basis of association. Thus, in Havana and Mexico City, first generation Spanish immigrants tend to prefer associations with persons from their own regions--Galicians with other persons from Galicia, Asturians with others from Asturias, and so on (Kenny, 1961b; Kenny, 1962).

Italian immigrants in New York City tend to congregate along village lines and a sort of "brotherhood" exists between males from the same village and series of obligations could be realized from this special relationship (Glazer and Moynihan, 187).

Egyptian peasants, when immigrating to Cairo, will often "seek out well-known 'successes' from their village to give them employment (Ubu-Lughod, 395)." These village "kinsmen" are well-known in the village and feel a special obligation to perform this service. In the Egyptian example, the tendency for immigrant settlement in the same section of Cairo is also noted (Ubu-Lughod, 397).

Ukranians prefer to marry spouses not only from just the available Ukrainian immigrant population, but even show a marked preference for persons from the same home village as their own (Anderson and Anderson, 163).

Oscar Lewis indicated that kinship ties tended to increase in the urban environment and that the Latin American compadrazco was still practiced with members of the same village (Lewis, 1964:1). A similar system of village oriented associative ties is also demonstrated in his recent work on Puerto Ricans in New York and San Juan (Lewis, 1966).

Research on American Indian groups shows that a tokoro-mon relationship may also exist on the reservation in the form of acculturated individuals preferring to associate with each other in preference to choosing acquaintances and friends among unacculturated Indians (Bruner, 1956:614-617). In this case, the patterns of association are not determined by locality, but, rather by interest. However, since common locality among immigrants often coincides with common interests (Glazer and Moynihan, 17), the two phenomena are clearly related. In studies of American Indians in an urban setting (Ablon, Kemnitzer, Swett, Graves, 1964) there is a marked tendency among Indians to seek out their tokoro-mon rather than other possible Indian choices. Of course, in the absence of persons coming from the same actual town or reservation, Indians will turn to other Indians before they will generally choose their friends among whites. While there are some historical reasons for this (Ablon), this sort of preference is also found among tribes settling in North Sumatra urban areas (Bruner, 1961), Swedes (Lindberg), Greeks (Saloutos, 1964) and Poles (Schermerhorn) settling in the United States as well as Italians in Chicago (Vecoli), Kentucky mountaineers in Ohio (Brown, Schwarzweller, and Mangalam, 1963) and Lebanese in West Africa (Creet).

CHAPTER V

THE ROLE OF INSTITUTIONAL PATHWAYS

Both formal and informal institutions are formed and used by immigrant groups to assist in their adaptation.

In addition to the tokoro-mon, the immigrant will often have assistance in his struggle for adaptation from various sorts of institutions. Three of these types of institutions might be (1) ethnic taverns and boarding houses, (2) voluntary associations, and (3) tokoro-mon connected recruitment for specific ethnic-based occupations.

Among an immigrant group lacking these types of institutions, the loss and subsequent damage has been noted by researchers (Martin, 294).

Ethnic Taverns

Ethnic taverns along with boarding houses, have been mentioned especially in terms of American Indian adjustment to American cities (Kemnitzer, 1964; Swett). Often, these "Indian" bars will be the first place an immigrant will seek out for finding tokoro-mon or employment and housing. The role of the city tavern for immigrant groups in general has been well documented as a function of neighborhood social organization and urban "community life (Richards)." The so-called "ethnic bar" and its functions is also examined in a general work on tavern behavior in general (Cavan). The functional equivalent of the Western tavern serving liquor in a Middle Eastern setting is the coffee shop.

> Many an Egyptian coffee shop is run by a villager to serve men from that particular village. News of the village is exchanged, mutual assistance for employment is given, and the venture more resembles a closed club than a commercial enterprise (Abu-Lughod, 397).

Workers seeking to establish such a regularity cross-culturally should be aware of the type of leisure-time social meeting places of their respective peoples. For circum-mediterranean peoples, it would, as in the example above, be the coffee shop that is the functional equivalent for the Western tavern. In both the tavern and the coffee shop used here, rarely is the main purpose of the establishment merely the consumption of the beverage or food sold there (at least, for the patrons). It is, rather, a meeting place which may be defined along associational lines of locality or ethnic origin where immigrants come to seek assistance and support in their new environments.

Voluntary Associations

Various types of "horizontal social ties (Potter, 380)" or voluntary associations are also founded by many ethnic groups for their mutual assistance in their adopted surroundings.[11] Some of these voluntary associations may have only a monetary motive in mind, such as those reported for India (Anderson) and the West Indies (Geertz). But most make as their primary function, at least in the first generation, the assisting of the immigrant in his adaptation.

The voluntary association has also been termed a "parallel ethnic institution" assisting its members "to be better citizens" in their new environment (Broom and Kitsuse, 45). Such groups function to "unite urbanites for shared interests which on the peasant scene are inherent in locality or kinship groups (Anderson and Anderson, 167), though they may begin only to perpetuate the home area's language and customs such as the Polish-American "Dom Polski (Schermerhorn, 412-414)." American immigrant groups are very well known for such groups (Handlin, 1966), but they appear to be a feature of immigrant settlements in other countries as well.

The services of such groups often include:

> ... consultant services where established members and non-members alike wrote to ask for help and advice on personal problems ranging from their difficulties in bureaucratic paper-work and the finding of employment to problems of health and family relations. Library loan services were established. Newspapers were founded. Seasonal activities were organized and halls were made available for weddings, social meetings, lectures, concerts and French language instruction. Women's sewing circles and welfare organizations complimented men's choirs and cooperatives. Eventually, sickness and unemployment help was given and steps taken to establish old people's homes (Anderson and Anderson, 162).

These services "protect migrants from the shock of anonmie," in their new surroundings (Abu-Lughod, 396). Often, such voluntary associations are good indicators of immigrant settlement for the researcher, such as in the Egyptian example, in addition to their assistance to the immigrant.

> The formal associations founded for and developed by migrants are important, directly, in the dynamics of rural to urban adaptatio, but are even more important indirectly, since their location and distribution in the city offer the only [emphasis hers] evidence as to where migrants settle in Cairo (Abu-Lughod, 389).

The importance of these benevolent societies tends to be greatest during the initial stages of adaptation (Embre, 407), such as the Japanese-American Kumi. Though one student has concluded that not all immigrants use the services of these voluntary associations, I feel that a close examination of her discussion of them reveals that they provide transitional support for immigrants who, upon establishing their own way, leave the associations.

> Through it [the village benevolent society] many migrants receive moral support from their compatriots as well as insurance against the insecurities of urban life, that is, isolation in poverty, sickness and death. It is unlikely, however, that more than 100,000 migrants are involved in these associations, while it will be recalled that their number exceeded 600,000 [up to] 1947. Thus, even if those associations are important to the persons they serve, they fall short of absorbing most migrants (Abu-Lughod, 397).

Various sorts of these associations are also reported, in the American context, for Italians (Glazer and Moynihan, 194; Vecoli), Greeks (Saloutos, 1964) and Swedes (Lindberg) in the United States. There is also a substantial literature for voluntary associations in Africa (Little). Voluntary associations, established on the basis of common village, are reported for Toba Batak in North Sumatra and function much as described above (Bruner, 1961:509).

American Indian immigrants to United States urban centers often establish such groups to aid in adaptation and appear to be more of a social nature (Kemnitzer, 1964; Swett). These groups organize "pow-wows" and promote what one student has termed "pan-Indianism (Ablon, 299)."

Spanish immigrants in Cuba and Mexico City have tended to establish their associations based upon the region or province from which they came and clearly are designed to promote understanding between the immigrant and his new culture (Kenny, 1961b:87), though it tended to be "later [after the beginnings of adaptation when they] took on a multi-purpose cultural aspect (Kenny, 1962:171)." For these, as well as other societies of this type in other contexts, actual assistance and encouragement for emigration from the home country would be provided through the association (Kenny, 1962:171). In Mexico City there are well over half a hundred of these associations, some of which represent splinter groups from the same region who have separated because of different political feelings regarding the home country (Kenny, 1962:173). Polish voluntary associations in the United States also split over political differences (Schermerhorn).

For Spaniards in Mexico City, elaborate insurance and health plans exist along with special hospitals for members and represent a well developed form of this type of association (Kenny, 1962:174). Developed though they might be (but not without parallels in other areas, mind you), I feel that the evidence presented above does not warrant his assertion that such voluntary associations "are a peculiar product of the overseas Spaniard (Kenny, 1962:174)," but, rather, a typical feature of most immigrant settlements.

Tokoro-mon Occupational Recruitment

Often assistance to immigrants will be a combination of tokoro-mon and possibly voluntary associations, but tied emphatically with the occupations typical of a given group, when such occupational specialization exists. Thus, it is a common feature of a voluntary association to assist in the employment of its immigrant constituents, though this is usually in a general fashion relying upon the occupations of the already established members. I would term such assistance as an "informal employment agency." The term "agency" is used since members of a given group will not always bring over immigrants to work for only themselves, but will often supply labor to other members of their ethnic group or even to members of the dominant culture in this fashion. References to this activity as it relates to voluntary associations has already been related above.

Clearly, the Lebanese "stranger-enclave" of West Africa conducts its immigration on this basis. Lebanese are brought over through relatives or tokoro-mon with their future role in the immigrant community occupational heirarchy already largely planned (Creet, 81-82).

What distinguishes this third and probably less prevalent type of adaptational institution is that it is specifically directed to employment and, as with the Lebanese case reported above, to a specific occupation or level of occupation. Often, an ethnic or immigrant group will specialize in a particular occupation and will offer transportation and assistance to other members from the home group if they will agree to work in the specified occupation upon arrival. In American cities, ethnicity, while it might sometimes have proven to be a hindrance, might also be the key to obtaining employment in some of the more ethnically related occupations (Handlin, 1956:3-4; Glazer and Moynihan; Bowers).

Sometimes these "employment agencies" will be formalized into actual business operations, but most often they are merely extensions of the voluntary associations and tokoro-mon institutions.

CHAPTER VI

CONSISTENT VALIDATION FOR ADAPTATION

Adaptation follows repeated validation on the part of the immigrant group. The manner in which this validation is to be carried out is largely provided by such aids as the tokoro-mon and the various formal and informal institutions listed in Chapter V. This chapter will mainly consider the types of problems most often encountered among immigrant groups.

Adaptation largely rests with the resident population, whereas "validation is the empirical test of the individuals' achieved acculturation (Broom and Kitsuse, 44)." Thus, while the immigrant group may strive to constantly prove themselves, the resident population by denying "access to participation in the dominant institutions (Broom and Kitsuse, 48)," can prevent successful adaptation from occurring (Spiro, 1245).

I intend to look at four recurring factors affecting the desire for validation and the degree of assimilation: (1) the size of the immigrant group and who it competes with occupationally, (2) the importance of "racial" markers, (3) "vertical" (Ginger) occupational and residential mobility as indicators of an advanced state of adaptation and as a sign of validation, and (4) intermarriage with the surrounding groups as an indicator of adaptation. This chapter will conclude the sequential aspect of my theory of migration and adaptation. Chapter VII is offered as an additional comment of a descriptive nature on immigrant groups whose first language is different from that of the inhabitants of their new environment.

Lest the reader feel that I am saying, above and in what is to follow, that it is the immigrant who is the only one affected in the processes I have examined, I would like to make it clear that this is not the case, as I have indicated in my note above regarding transculturation. Herskovits, in commenting upon non-Western peoples who have been colonized by Europeans, notes:

> It is doubtful, as a matter of fact, whether the native peoples of the world, by and large, have taken over much more of Euro-american culture than the Western world has borrowed from them (Herskovits, 176).

Thus, acculturation affects both the "receiver" and the "donor." Urbanization affects both the urban dweller and the immigrant. Immigration affects both the immigrant and the "natives."

The problems involved in validation are on-going ones and continue to plague the immigrant population until a more or less final effort at adaptation is achieved and this effort is recognized by the resident group and they cease to be defined as "immigrants." Validation may also be seen as the process by which the immigrant understands and acquires the "ethnomethodology" of the native group (Garfinkel).

In order to find out, for a given immigrant-resident situation what sorts of acts are required for validation, one:

... should study intensively the ways [their emphasis] that the acculturated patterns of behavior are used by the group undergoing change and the contexts [their emphasis] in which they are used (Broom and Kitsuse, 44).

There is, below, an assumption that an immigrant group wishes to adapt for purposes of settlement. This is not always the case for a variety of reasons. Lebanese in West Africa appear to be quite content with their enclavement in African society and do not appear to be willing to fully adapt (Creet). Jews in New York City often show a great reticence to adaptation and are often referred to as living in a "gilded ghetto (Glazer and Moynihan, 180)." In fact, for immigrants to the United States, it has been pointed out that there appears to be "some central tendency in the National ethos which structures people ... into groups of different status and character (Glazer and Moynihan, 291)." While this may be a feature of American society, evidence presented above would appear to support the idea that it is a general tendency, to greater and lesser degrees, of human society as a whole.

There is, of course, the possibility that a group might continually validate their acceptance of the dominant life style but not consciously have adaptation in mind. Their interests might be of a more limited nature. Among the non-immigrant North Alaskan Eskimos, the White Man's ways are mimiced, but only when Eskimos are in contact with whites. It is done to procure and secure employment (Chance, 375). The proof of the limited use of validation is that when they return to their native villages away from their employment in the white world, at the end of the day or on holidays, they shift to their old Eskimo patterns (Chance, 375). Changes, however, are occurring in their life style on a subtle level and "the Eskimos have become much more dependent on items of Western technology and social institutions (Chance, 375)." So, even if validation is not undertaken with the purpose of adaptation, it is likely to be the end result, regardless of its premeditated purpose.

Immigrant Population Size and Occupation Competition

The size of the immigrant group and with whom they compete occupationally has an important bearing on the degree of validation required and the rate of adaptation. Early Greek immigrants to the United States were few in number and were mostly professional or skilled individuals (Saloutos, 1964:22-23). Many of these Greeks were successful and drew little attention to themselves. It was only later when they came in larger numbers, did they become a "problem." In fact, for United States immigration in general, it might be noted that the Immigration Act of 1924, based upon national origins, was a response to the tremendous numbers of unskilled persons entering that country in the late nineteenth and especially the early twentieth century (Glazer and Moynihan, 289).

Japanese in Chicago relate their success partially to their small numbers and relatively high degree of training (Caudill and DeVos, 1107). On the other hand, the large numbers of Toba Batak in Medan, North Sumatra, have contributed to their success (Bruner, 1961:519). Part of this, of course, might be due to the lack of an actual homogeneous "dominant group" in the city (Bruner, 1961:520). Their awareness of their tribal ethnic identity is strong at this point and so it would seem that this lack of a dominant culture might retard the adaptation of the various groups.

23

American Indians in United States urban settings come in relatively small numbers (Swett; Kemnitzer, 1964; Graves). But they often compete with relatively low status groups for employment owing often to their lack of skills. Of course, for such a culturally varied heterogeneous group as the migrant American Indian, few generalizations may be actually made. Indians vary considerably in their degree of success and degree of preparation (Graves, 1965; Hirabayashi and Willard; Martin) just as some so-called "peasant migrants" vary in their degree of preparation and ability for adaptation (Abu-Lughod; Potter; Qualey; Halpern, 1964). But, aside from these factors of preparation, discussed more fully in Chapter I, the size of an immigrant group on the whole has an effect on how the resident group will conceptualize the immigrant. In New York City, ethnic groups were seen to have been formed and conceptualized as much by the group's own self-identity as it was by out-group pressures (Glazer and Moynihan).

"Racial" Markers

Racial markers have their effect on the ability of a group to adapt, especially when these racial markers are highly visible.[12] One need only mention the case of the Negro in the United States to see how "visible" race can affect efforts at validation.[13] For some groups, racial markers do not appear to hinder their acceptance (Caudill and DeVos). Whether or not Japanese in Chicago will be able to finally adapt is another question. Below, I make as a precondition to total adaptation intermarriage. I would say that visible racial markers most always have an affect upon intermarriage and therefore final adaptation, as noted above, no matter how hard the group validates its acceptance of dominant life style. At least, this appears to have been for most of human history, though some might argue that such an attitude is not as prevalent today.[14] Whether the attitude is disappearing or not does not discount the fact that most immigrant groups to any society who have had visible racial markers have encountered difficulty in adaptation.

Occupational and Residential Mobility

Vertical occupational mobility and residential mobility indicate validation as well as successfully progressing adaptation. In the early stages of adaptation, a sort of enclavement is usual. Peasants coming into Cairo often continue to live for a while directly near the bus or train terminal at which they first arrived. There are, "within the city of Cairo ... numerous sub-areas whose physical and social characteristics closely approximate the villages of the countryside (Abu-Lughod, 388). So, peasants coming from the north tend to live in northern Cairo and peasants coming from the south tend to live in the southern part of the city (Abu-Lughod, 390). This would indicate a low degree of adaptation in my theory. Italians in New York City also tend to congregate along these lines and students today note how little have the boundary limits of the Italian community changed since the early part of this century (Glazer and Moynihan, 187).

Work on ethnic groups in Australia also reveals a positive correlation between residential concentration of a given group and degree of adaptation (Jones).

There are two kinds of occupational mobility--vertical and horizontal (Ginger, 235). A person moving from unskilled job to unskilled job is exhibiting horizontal occupational mobility. However, a person moving from an unskilled job to a semi-skilled job is exhibiting vertical occupational mobility. It is this latter type of occupational mobility with which I am concerned.

24

Occupational mobility implies not only that the immigrant group itself is trying to adapt, but that the resident group is allowing it (Ianni).

Occupational mobility (moving up the "occupational ladder") is tied to residential mobility.

> Thus, if the occupational structure of an ethnic group is expanding toward the higher status occupations, and if mobility aspirations are strong enough, we might expect a subsequent advance in residential mobility as acculturation proceeds. ... Consequently, acculturation becomes a necessary although not always sufficient preliminary to acceptance in such neighborhoods (Ianni, 71).

The relationship, then, is reciprocal and is an indicator of community feelings about a given immigrant group. "Resistances encountered by a group in occupational mobility lead to consequent inability to advance in residential mobility (Ianni, 71)." Occupational mobility is, of course, often reliant upon merely the manpower needs of a community.

Intermarriage

Lastly, when the immigrant groups have been accepted occupationally and residentially, the ultimate proof of acceptance and adaptation and the end to the immigrant's status as "immigrant" is intermarriage.[15] Again, as with the other points regarding validation above, this is dependent upon a give and take relationship between the immigrant and the resident. The immigrant has to seek to want to marry outside of his ethnic group and the resident has to want to allow this move. I would postulate that rarely does intermarriage take place without first occupational and residential mobility being established. Information about ethnic groups in Australia tends to confirm this (Jones), as does data on immigrant groups in the United States (Glazer and Moynihan).

Such factors as religion and race do enter into marriage choices, of course. Religion "may serve to accelerate or retard the general acculturative process (Spiro, 1246)." Religion and race become problems only if there are no residents of the same category. Thus, immigrant Jews may marry American Jews or Catholic Italians may marry Catholic Americans, in the United States context. In North Sumatra, there is difficulty because of the division between Moslems and Christians, which may even cross-cut "ethnic" lines (Bruner, 1961:519).

With the completion of this final step, adaptation becomes complete and the immigrant ceases to be. Following this sort of mixing, "ethnicity" may become largely of interest and preference. "The ethnic group is not surely a biological phenomenon (Glazer and Moynihan, 16)." After intermarriage has occurred, distinguishing markers become less and less noticeable and if the idea of separateness is going to be continued to be used, for example, as the basis of a club or other social activity, then the inclusion or rejection of persons in such an "ethnic group" will largely be a matter of arbitrary decision. So, "the American descendants of immigrants diverge markedly from the people of the Old Country (Glazer and Moynihan, 12)." This does not mean that after adaptation, there is any attempt to return to a separated status. They may continue to refer to themselves as residents rather than immigrants, but, possibly for purposes of buttressing their own sense of identity, also call attention to their ethnic identity. Many social clubs in the United States operate in this manner. Descendants of Fulani "immigrants" to Nigeria of some years ago, for example, still think of themselves as Fulani, though they have intermarried and can scarcely speak Fulani. They use the Fulani connection as a sanction for their political power (Ames).

This is not "nativism" which is usually the quest for status and identity self-validation in the face of failure at adaptation. It is, rather, the constructing of associative ties along self-perceived "ethnic ties" generally for purposes of social intercourse. This tendency will often occur among third generation members and might be termed, "the principle of third generation interest. What the son wishes to forget, the grandson wishes to remember (Hanson, 260)." In New York City, ethnic groups may often be characterized thus:

> Concretely, persons think of themselves as members of that group, with that name; they are thought by others as members of that group, with that name; and most significantly, they are linked to other members of the group by new attributes that the original immigrants would never have recognized as identifying their group, but which nevertheless serve to mark them off, by more than simply name and association in the third generation and even beyond (Glazer and Moynihan, 13).

I have not included this "principle of third generation interest" as a separate point under validation, but have tied it into intermarriage as a sign of significant and advanced adaptation. The data I have appears to apply to immigrant groups in the United States, in general.

CHAPTER VII

LANGUAGE DIFFERENCES

This last chapter relates only to those immigrants whose first language differs from the language of the resident group. For nearly all of the groups on whom I have the relevant data a report that language is one of the more difficult drawbacks to adaptation is present. An interesting phenomenon connected with language differences is that the second generation children of the immigrants will often act as mediators between their "foreign" immigrant parents and the larger resident community and may even take on the role of instructing their parents in the ways of the resident community.

Though not made explicit for some groups, language difficulties are very common among immigrant groups to the United States (Saloutos, 1964; Lindberg). The Lebanese in West Africa, who are not interested in losing their separateness, learn the local trade language only for business purposes (Creet).

In measuring the degree of acculturation or adaptation for a given group, it has been shown that a good indicator is always which language is spoken as the "home" language (Bruner, 1956:618-621).

A function of this language problem is that the immigrant's children often go to schools conducted by the resident culture where they are subjected to the changing influences of education. For Polish-Americans the home lost its educational influence upon the second generation Poles and they often became, by virtue of their schooled familiarity with American culture, the ones to whom the parents looked for advice in dealing with the resident culture (Schermerhorn, 417).

A general survey of American ethnic groups reveals that the tendency that "it is the children who teach the new culture to their parents (Spiro, 1247)" appears to be prevalent among most groups.

Some authors have postulated that this condition results in a loss of parental authority (Schermerhorn), but I do not feel that this necessarily must be the case.

In Part I, I have presented and detailed six major parts of a sequential theory of migration and adaptation. The theoretical unity of urbanization, acculturation, and immigration under this rubric was established and my investigations to this point were organized with this unity in mind.

In the next part, these postulates will be applied to my data on Basque-Americans, with some side reference to Basques in Mexico City.

PART II

BASQUE MIGRATION AND ADAPTATION TO THE UNITED STATES

INTRODUCTION

Below, I propose to draw upon printed sources and my own field notes on the Basques to describe Basque migration to and adaptation in the United States.[16] It is my intention to test the sequential theory I developed in Part I on this material. Because of this limited goal, some of the long history of the Basques, their culture and their migrations will not be included, for example, in Chapter I regarding cultural background.

A comprehensive view of Basques in the American West is offered by a French Basque priest who visited many Basque-American communities in the early nineteen-fifties (Gachiteguy). While some doubt has been expressed as to the reliability of his statistical speculations, I do not feel that this criticism is warranted since a sociological study was not his intent. He sought to survey. He sought to provide some picture of Basque life in America, or, as he says, to discover:

> Cet entrecroisement d'événements heureux et tragiques, la complexité
> de la marque du Far-West sur le caractere de mon père, m'ont toujours
> laisse perplexe au sujet du pays des Peaux-Rouges. Les événements
> m'ont permis depuis lors l'étude detaillée de ce pays des rêves de
> mon enfance. La voici, a l'intention de ceux que hantent les memes
> rêves (Gachiteguy, 1).

The picture he offers is fairly complete, though serious errors exist with respect to his information about the Idaho area. The social science work on the Basques in this country, with the exception of the one brief article extracted from a doctoral dissertation (Edlefsen, 1950), are all references which are unpublished.

The first thesis done on the Basques offers a good community study approach to the problem of social change[17] (Gaiser, 1944). The next study completed with a sociological outlook bore a great resemblance to the first one, especially in matters of style and organization. Thus, certain comparisons are possible between the two, though the two communities are in close proximity to each other (Edlefsen, 1948). The first student of the Basques, Gaiser, intends to complete a longitudinal study of the same area he worked in over twenty years past (Gaiser, 1966).

Each of the studies shown in the bibliography in the appendix under "Unpublished Sources" contains some words about the history of the Basques and their migrations to the Western Hemisphere. The best tracing of this, however, was done in conjunction with a study of the Basque "sheepherder bills" (Nason).

For the brief background information I give on Basque immigration, I intend to rely mostly on secondary sources.[18] When appropriate, in the rest of the examination, I will turn to my field notes. Chapter II in this part draws heavily from an examination of Basque migrations to Columbia (Kasdan).

During my field work with the Basques in this country, I did have occasion to do a brief survey of the Basques living in Mexico City. I will not emphasize any data on the Basques who have emigrated to areas other than the United States. Those Basques living in the Philippines, Australia, and in the very large and active colonies of South America and Cuba present quite different problems in their adaptation and the time depth of these colonies generally is much greater than that of the United States settlements (Figure 1).[19]

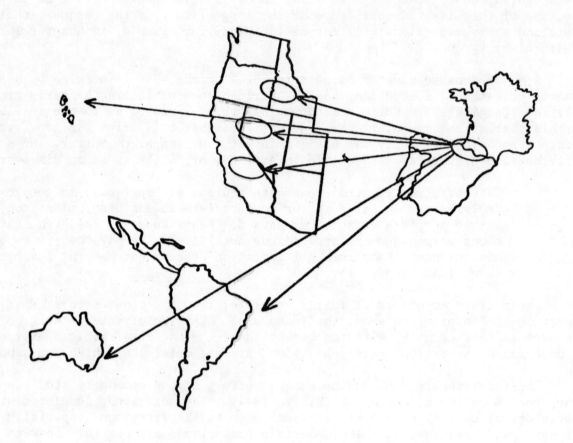

Figure 1

Basque Immigration in the World

(Major Areas)

CHAPTER I

THE CULTURAL BACKGROUND OF THE BASQUES

With the exception of a few passes at either end, the Pyrenees form an effective divider to cut the Iberian peninsula off from the rest of Europe. The homeland of the Basques is known to them as Euskal-Herria or by its political name Euzkadi and is in the western end of these mountains, which rise abruptly from the plains of Aquitania and are contiguous with the maturely dissected Cantabrian range in Spain. The Ebro River serves to mark the western boundary of what the Spanish Basques claim as their own today, but the boundaries in France and in the Pyrenees are more difficult to fix. The "core culture" of the Basques is based in the small valleys that dissect the massif.[20] Owing to the crystalline core of the mountains, and its glacial history, watersheds are fairly complex and the present Spanish French political boundary dissecting the Basque country bears little relationship to either cultural or transhumance[21] patterns.

The combination of steep slopes, spurs and valleys makes for local variations in ecology and tends to magnify them. Sunlight differs according to the side of the valley, and often determines settlement patterns, while the perpetually shady side is left to forest and pasture, the sunny side being intensively cultivated.

In discussing the cultural patterns of the European Basques, writers have spoken both pro and con to the question of sheepherding in the Basque country. Transhumance, much like it is practiced in the West by the Basques, has been a feature of Basque life for centuries and the herding of sheep is familiar to many Basques (B. Estornes-Lasa). This question is explored in more detail below with reference to one of the more detailed examinations of this question (Gomez-Ibáñez).

The Basques, as a people, might be best seen as a group of closely related tribes, rather than as a culturally homogeneous group. Each province has its own customs and forms of speech, as well as folk-defined character uniqueness. On the Spanish side, the Basques provinces are Vizcaya, Alava, Navarra, and Guipuzcoa, with the French provinces being Soule, Labourd and Basse-Navarre.[22]

The Basque family structure is that of the famillie-souche or stem family (Caro Baroja, 1958:154). Aside from the animals, inhabitants of the typical timber and stone or packed earth house include: (1) grandparents; (2) master and mistress of the house, one of whom is the eldest offspring of the grandparents; (3) their unmarried children; (4) unmarried siblings of the master or mistress (whoever is the eldest); and (5) servants. Servants, if they exist, are for the household chores and are treated as members of the family (Caro Baroja, 1958:263). The listing above also represents the heirarchy of power in the household.

Traditionally, primogeniture rules and even attempts on the French and Spanish sides have failed to dilute the power of this rule. More will be said about this system and its tremendous effect on Basque life in Chapter II.

Women enjoy a position of equal respect among the Basques. So note-worthy is the magnitude of this respect, that the early geographer Strabo, in the first century A.D., severely criticized them for this. Marriages tend to be arranged among prospective spouses and women will often work in the fields along with men, preparing the ground for planting and harvesting. The division of labor runs something like this:

Within the house, all the labor, except that of feeding the sheep, can be said to be the occupation of the woman. In labor in the field, both sexes participate. The occupations proper to the men are: the care of sheep, cattle, horses and wool, feeding them, building fences in the fields. Those of the women are: preparing meals for the family, washing and mending clothes, care of chickens, buying objects for the kitchen, sale of the vegetables, eggs, etc. The young boys customarily collect the sheep, and drive cattle to pasture and guard them (Barandiaran, 1948:183).

Following a usual Catholic pattern, divorce is usually not allowed. My informants have mentioned to me that the remarriage of a divorced person is attended by much noise making and harassment in the community. Since Catholicism is the religion of the Basques,[23] you may also expect some general patterns to be true that are found among other Catholic populations (Douglass, 1966).

Two settlement patterns are prevalent in the rural areas: nuclear and "plurinuclear" settlements, in the valleys and along streams, and isolated homesteads on the slopes. These are organized into vecindades, or neighborhoods, with definite boundaries based on a single valley and surrounding pastures. Fields are on the flow or lower slopes of the valley along with permanent habitation. Villages contain a few nuclear houses, with generally surrounding satellite isolated homesteads. Sometimes the vecindades are only isolated homesteads with no town center.

The regulation of common land use, settlement of civil and criminal cases, and the negotiations with other vecinidades over disputed land is carried out by local councils or juntas. These bodies are sometimes termed "anteiglesias," to distinguish them from those of royal or seigniogal origin (Caro Baroja, 1958:105). Membership and election varies: some allow all male citizens, others only freeholder, councilmen choose their successors in other juntas, although freehold membership is probably more common. Lawyers, clergy and nobility are barred from membership. When the freeholder is a woman, she chooses a male member of her household to represent her in some cases, in other cases she sits in on the junta herself.

Woodcutting and hunting are among the activities regulated in command lands, but by far the most important village activity is sheepherding. Other communal activities come about as a result of membership in the vecinidad, some of these dating back to codes of the tenth century. Such codes or fueros are not to define the relationship of citizen to ruler, primarily, but also citizen to citizen and include recommendations of penalties (Galindez, 1957; Galindez, 1947). A newcomer to the vecindad has to be elected vecino by the other citizens and has to pay a tax before pursuing his trade--in many cases he has to be of Basque origin on both sides. Vecinos are bound in networks of mutual aid: they serve each other as witnesses in legal matters, perform marriage and funeral rites, and cooperate in reciprocal work parties. Informal social controls include ritual harassment (the charivari) for deviant vecinos,[24] denial of vecino privileges and, even banishment.

Three categories of land ownership are recognized: (1) privately owned land belonging to the house, and used for agriculture, (2) communal pasturage and forest belonging to the inhabitants of a vecinidad, (3) pasturage and forest held in common by several vecinidades. In addition, there is a traditional funeral path (see Douglass, 1966) which must be maintained. Though previously much land was owned by absentee landlords, since the nineteenth century land ownership has passed into the hands of the inhabitants (Caro Baroja, 1944:33).

Traditional Basque society has been stratified since the tenth century. The fueros (privileges), codified at that time, recognize three classes of men: (1) hombresricos, owning much land, who elected a king from among them, (2) infanzones of limited wealth and land, (3) hidalgos, including artisans, peasants, and merchants. The status of hidalgo or "nobleman" was only granted formally to the provinces of Vizcaya and Guipuzcoa (Gallop, 15), but many Basques make a point of the equality and nobility of all of the Basques, especially if these informants are encountered outside of the Basque country!

In addition to these classes, an outcaste group, called agotes, cagots is recognized. They are sometimes thought of as a "race" and are often convenient scapegoats along with, to a lesser degree, the gypsies of the area.

The Basque social world consists of family, vecinos, neighboring vecinos, other Basques and non-Basques. Family obligations are reported in sources as those having to do with claims that returned family members make for shelter. The next strongest obligation is to the "first neighbor."[25] They may also be some confradias or other cross-vecindad groups to whom the Basque may owe some support.

The Basques have managed to retain their uniqueness as a group for some time. All of the above methods for maintaining solidarity, plus the prohibition on exogamous marriages have contributed to a unique physical type for the Basque though, by no means is this consistent through all the Basque country. Ripley notes that the Basques are generally dolichocephalic and French Basques are generally brachycephalic and the so-called "ideal" Basque facial type, occurring in about fifteen percent of the population of an area near the international boundary, is "upside-down" to the Cro-Magnon facial structure--pointed chin, narrow malars, and wide temporal measurement (Ripley, 79-83). Other descriptions of Basques vary, but the central fact remains that most Basques are able to tell who their brethren are just by looking at them. What sorts of clues are used in this identification process are unknown to me, but almost all of my informants report that identification can most often be made.

Another writer describes the "ideal" face thus: forehead straight or slightly sloping, browridges weak or absent, nasion depression slight or absent, nose thin or aquiline with thin tip, forehead broad, mid-face narrow, mandible extremely slender and narrow, and chin pointed (Coon).

Blood group studies[26] based on 383 Ss (Chalmers et al., 1949) and 161 Ss (Alderdi et al., 1957), and the more recent general survey (Marquer) seem to confirm the pattern of high O and exceptionally low B frequencies. These patterns have also been tested on Basques living outside of continental Basque country in America (Gray), in Chile (Vacarro et al.), and Argentina (Etcheverry, 1949). Regarding the extraordinary feature of the Rh negative prevalence (as high as 65 percent in one study), an author conjectured that,

> ... el pueblo vasco seria la fuente originero Rh negativa, a
> partir de la cual se ha llegado mezolas con otros pueblos
> predominante Rh positiva, a la distribucion actual de ambos
> propriedades en los habitantes del oeste europeo (Etcheverry,
> 1959:83).

In order to determine if indeed a Raza Vasca[27] does exist as some contend, comparative studies have been undertaken (Pons, Moulinier) as well as studies of other aspects of the body such as the cranium (Riquet, Morant, Aranzadi).

The claim of uniqueness rests--the nature and significance of that uniqueness is another matter. A more thorough review of the problem has been handled elsewhere (Estornes Lasa, IV).

In terms of linguistic similarities, I have elsewhere reviewed the range of such comparative studies which stretch all the way from calling Basques people from Atlantis to comparing them with American Indian languages.[28] Tovar (1957:38) cites resemblances in the passivity of the verb denoting the object, that correspond in similar forms in Georgian and Abkhaz; comparison of vocabulary shows similarities in words relating to cattle-raising and agriculture, but none in words relating to metals and metal-working. A recent investigator has noted his preference for a Basque-Caucasion relationship, though he himself favors structural studies (Jon Bilbao, 1968).

Basque forms can be recognized in quotations in the tenth century manuscripts, but no written literature exists prior to the middle of the sixteenth century. A good case might be made for considering the Basques as a "pre-literate people." The Basques have no long tradition of literature, save for ecclesiastical documents, and no independent tradition of literature developed until the nineteenth century (Juan Bilbao). What has developed since then has been closely tied with the Basque nationalist movements (Juan Bilbao). But the real "literature" of the people is oral. It is the folktales and legends told by the older people and their poetry is the extemporaneous constructions of the Bertsolari, who is something like the Icelandic Skald with his "song duels" (Lecuona). The Basque language does not have its own alphabet, but uses a borrowed one from Europeans. A few of my informants have commented on this fact of the Basque being unwilling to write. They report cases of Basques leaving their families and going to the New World, staying away for forty years or longer and never writing letters to home. As an informant in Puerto Rico put it: "We Basques don't like to write much. We like to talk a lot, but not write."

There are a number of opinions about the nature of Basque character. Their ferocity and savagery appear to have attracted the attention of most early writers and it could be conjectured that these traits were recorded because of being questioned too intently by early investigators! (Gallop, 9-11). Later, one writer in the seventeenth century saw Basque traits as:

> Simplicity of spirit, scantiness of wit, reason, speech and manners; aptitude to be confidential secretaries, on account of their administrative precision and calligraphic skill; aptitude for seafaring; affection for wine and tendency to drunkenness; arrogant, coleric and impetuous humour (Caro Baroja, 1958:357).

A modern French writer saw that they were "more inclined to homicide and vengeance than larceny or pardon ... faithful to whatever they say ... I never saw anyone condemned in this parliament for stealing anything of importance (Ormond, 43)." Ortega y Gasset felt that "The Basque thinks that the mere fact of having been born and of being an individual gives him all the value that it is possible for one to have in this world (Ortega y Gasset, 25)."

It has been noted that "Basque history, considered in its broadest aspect, is the history of the independence of the Basque provinces, and of their gradual submission, not so much to the countries to which they offered allegiance, as to irresistible forces of time and progress (Gallop, 13)." Gradually, from the first

Carlist war, down to the Second Carlist War, and finally the Spanish Civil War, the Basques lost more and more of their autonomy. The connection between the outbreak of these wars and emigration has been made (Lhande). The details of this history are complex and not directly relevant here. Sources on the Civil War tend to be strongly partisan and the Basque side has been well presented (Steer, Astilarra). The story of the Basque Government in Exile, which still maintains delegations in various Latin American Countries, in Paris and in New York City, also has its early history available (Aguirre).

Emigration is a part of both Basque history and Basque social organization. The Basques have been active in the armies of Europe as mercenaries for centuries (Lhande). After the "official opening" of the Age of Discovery, the Basque participation on the side of Spain was extensive.[16] Their names appear and reappear in any chronicle of Spanish conquests in the New World (Ispizua).

Commentary in most works done on the Basques in this country confirm that they have a respect for authority grounded in their strong family structure (Gaiser; Edlefsen, 1948). One student, in assessing how the Basques have survived as a people, summarized these points from a study of the literature:

> Insistence on individual freedom, complemented by a predelection
> to formalization of cooperation in auto chthonous councils; locality
> as a first principle of family and vecindad, complemented by migra-
> tion and transhumance; conservatism in ideas, complemented by
> adaptability to stress; complementarity of the sexes; bravado,
> strength and agility emphasized as male values; conception of the
> world as a source of challenge, which one is bound to accept, and
> from which there is no retreat, of fellow Basques as people to be
> trusted, and of non-Basques as threats to liberty and privacy;
> interdependence of man, animate and inanimate beings; conception
> of life as essentially sombre. In addition, here is hypothesized
> a unified time sense, as expressed in the conservationist approach
> to nature, the emphasis on continuity of the family, strict primo-
> geniture, and permanent type construction (Kemnitzer, 1963:17).

Using Kemnitzer's summary of Basque personality traits, let us compare Basques with what are some traits of the American personality[29] to see how some convergence might occur:

> The dominant religious motif in the American middle class appears
> to revolve around the "Protestant Ethic," a value system in which
> is found, among other things, a strong individualistic orientation,
> a high premium put on personal effort and individual validation of
> status, and a strong sense of personal responsibility in religious
> as well as secular affairs (Cohen, 419).

An anthropological study of American character pointed to the strong emphasis placed upon self-reliance and independence (Mead). In fact, one investigator would even place this value as a central "core value" in American culture (Hsu). Modern technology and ethnic heterogeneity have apparently not weakened the pre-eminence of this trait (Riesman). I feel that Basque and the dominant American personality expectations converge and that Basque immigrants to the United States might be expected to be able to adapt reasonably well.

The pre-eminent role of emigration in Basque social structure is part and parcel of Chapter II.

CHAPTER II

PRESSURE TO SUCCEED FOR THE BASQUES

Many of the features pointed out above regarding Basque society might lead one to believe that it is static and highly resistant to change.

> Basque society fully meets the criteria of a traditional peasant society. ... The settlement pattern consists of nucleated villages with few houses; religion is a primary integrating force; there is family cultivation with specialists working at the specialties only on a part-time basis; production is through the use of hand tools; mobilization of labor byond the family is on a communal basis. ... It is hard to see why this combination of features should lead to the creation of entrepreneurs among the Basques when it stultifies such activities in other peasant societies. The Basques in fact are a classic example of a peasant group which has used every means to resist change including force (Kasdan, 348).

Along with the above themes, are also feelings of strong individuality and self-sufficiency--characteristics which do fit into the entrepreneurial pattern. A central feature of Basque society causes it to produce two classes of citizens-- those who have a place and those who do not. This central feature is closely tied with marriage rules and the system of primogeniture.[30]

> The basic unit of the Basque rural community is the family farm (casario), which is ideally a self-sufficient unit. ... Unmarried residents may make no claims of inheritance upon it. Both rules of inheritance and rules of marriage buttress the inviolability of the casario (Kasdan, 349-350).

The one who is allowed to honorably remain in the casario of the Basque community is the etxe jauna, or "lord of the house." This person is the eldest child of the family and may be either male or female.[31] The fueros prohibit a male heir from marrying a female heir, since the eldest daughter of a family may also inherit the casario. The rest of the siblings, then, are forced to one of six alternatives which have been open to them throughout most of Basque history:

1. Some are given payment in cash which they are expected to use in building an independent income, usually outside of the local community.

2. Some become indianos, immigrants to the New World, who will in theory return with fortunes made there.

3. Being highly orthodox Catholics, many Basques join religious orders or pursue other ecclesiastical careers.

4. A very small number may remain in their natal communities as artisans or shepherds.

5. Some become sailors, and today many are absorbed into industry, just as in the distant past many were absorbed in the armies of the reconquest and/or in the interior colonization attendant upon the expulsion of the Moors.

6. A small number remain celibate within their own casarios (Kasdan, 351).

Emigration became a substantial and expected part of Basque life early in their history and their involvement in Continental Europe and its affairs dates from the earliest histories of the area (Lhande). In the nineteenth century this emigration was mostly directed to various parts of the Western Hemisphere.

In some Pyrenean valleys of Navarre, male youths regularly become indianos, i.e., immigrate at an early age to the Americas, leaving their sisters behind para casa as heirs to the natal houses. The sisters will then marry returned indianos while their brothers return years later, presumably with an accumulated store of capital, and marry in the same vicinity women left para casa by their brothers (Kasdan, 350).

But, as seen in the general formulation of my theory above, the leaving of property to one heir either by primogeniture, ultimogeniture, or selection of the "ablest child," while it often sparked emigration, did not make for a particularly strong pressure to succeed. With the Basques, however, their strict primogeniture means that siblings know from an early age what their alternatives will be. It is reasonable to assume that these "disinherited" siblings "will develop different attitudes and personality characteristics than their sibling (in most cases a first-born son) who has his status as an heir defined by birth order (Kasdan, 352)."

Those who choose emigration as their means for securing an identity and prestige are a highly select group and the necessity they feel for succeeding is very high. Most of my informants reported on this felt need to succeed; to keep the Basque name (and their own family name, of course) good. It was unthinkable that a Basque émigre could return to his village without having succeeded in his immigration efforts. He had to adapt to life in his chosen new home, whether it be the United States, Canada, South America, or Australia.

At least two cases have come to my attention of émigres who made it known to their fellow Western American Basques that they did not feel that they could succeed--one committed suicide and the other has, over his years here, gradually stopped speaking to anyone. When the desire to return to the Basque country is absent, often a sort of listless anomie will set in. Such a case recently was reported for a Basque who had made his fortune in the United States and, upon returning to the Basque country, found that his betrothed had, in a most un-Basquelike manner, married another man. He now herds sheep in California, appears not to be interested in saving his money, and exhibits neither a desire to return to the Basque country, nor, for that matter, to better his position (Ron Taylor).

Moderate success has been observed by me in the majority of my informants, but extreme cases of success are well-known among members of the Basque community in first and second generation Basque-Americans. One of more well-known is the French Basque whose three sons (born in this country) have acquired positions as an editor of a University press, a prominent lawyer, and the governor of a Western state.

Also, well-known is the Spanish Basque who started out in a menial capacity in a Western gambling casino and now owns it! Their success in the Western sheep industry has been well detailed previously (Nason, Gomez-Itáñez). Almost all of these successes desire to return to the Basque country to "prove" themselves. These returns, if only for brief visits, are often very touching in their emotional intensity (Laxalt, 1957).

The retournee who seeks to remain in his village is not uncommon and "retournees" from "America" are found living in many Basque villages (Douglass, 1967). But, just as often, a Basque will return "to stay," in his native village and then repeat his immigration to his adopted land for a variety of reasons. One informant reported that her father had performed this shift seven times.[32]

While not explicitly the subject of this thesis, it must also be conjectured that there is equal pressure of a different sort exerted upon the etxe jauna. The expectations he must fulfill, while not of the entrepreneurial type, are nevertheless strong. One second-generation American informant reported that she, as the eldest of the family, even in the American context, was expected to succeed and made to feel very guilty when she did not live up to her parents' expectations.[33]

Certain parallels between the material above and that presented in Part I for Spaniards in Cuba and Mexico might be noted. Basques have, for the most part, been connected with Spanish colonial activities, though very high emigration rates, in terms or percentage, are also reported for the French Basque country (Lhande). Why is it that non-Basque Spanish do not exhibit some of the same strong drive to succeed? Though primogeniture does exist in some areas of Spain, it is not the general rule (Kasdan, 352). If a single heir is chosen, it is after the siblings have attained some age and so, I feel, does not equate itself with the bipolar differential patterns of socialization reported above.

I would say that the Basques have felt a definite pressure to succeed and that this has, plus the important opportunity for entrepreneurial activity afforded by their participation in the sheep industry (Gomez-Ibáñez, Kelly, Nason), contributed to their success in this country. By adapting themselves to this ecological niche, with its attendant minimal social intercourse, they also were less in a position to be in conflict with the surrounding Anglo culture.

CHAPTER III

KIN AND HOME-BASED ASSOCIATIVE TIES FOR THE BASQUES

Most sources on Basque immigration to the United States note that early immigrants came to "California," meaning most of the Western states (Edlefsen, Gaiser). This is not surprising since the Basque participation in the life of Spanish California (the territory taking in most of the southwest prior to the United States purchase of it) was great (Nason).

The Basque settlements of the West (New York and Florida settlements are somewhat special) tend to be divided into three zones of influence and association.

The first zone takes in southwestern Idaho and Oregon and is where most of the research on Basque-Americans has been made (McCullough, Edlefsen, Gaiser). The area is almost entirely populated by persons either from Vizcava or of Vizcayan descent (Edlefsen).

The second zone is northern Nevada and, to some extent, northeastern California. This area received some of the first immigrants who left California and made their way to the northwest. Their colonies center around the Nevada towns of Elko, Reno, Winnemucca, and the California towns of Alturas and Cedarville. Many of the Spanish and French Basques in this area (Gachiteguy) first started their lives in the United States on the coast of California, but then comprised a secondary migration, taking them to where they live now. Within this zone, people know each other and, to some extent, mediate between the Basques of zone one (the most publicized Basque festival is held in Elko) and zone three.

The third zone is the largest in land area and, possibly, in population as well. This does not, however, prevent a sort of minimal feeling of association among the occupants. It is mainly composed of French Basques (Challet) and comprises the states of California, southern Nevada (Gardner-ville, Ely), Utah, Arizona, New Mexico, Colorado and Wyoming. This third zone is "held together" by a French Basque priest, traditionally under the jurisdiction of the Bishop of Bayonne, whose task it is to travel almost constantly throughout the year from his Fresno base to visit with and give Mass to Basques in these areas. He also serves as an informal messenger between kin and friends often even carrying photographs and gifts between Basques in these areas.

These zones are not hard and fast divisions, for some overlap, either by kin or other home-based associative ties will exist. But, generally speaking, Basques living in La Puente, California or San Francisco will not have a clear idea of how other Basques live in Idaho and visa versa. One such overlap, for example, is the somewhat regular transport of chorizos[34] from an Idaho meat company to a San Francisco Basque restaurant. But, within these zones, people will know each other and be from similar parts of the Basque Country.[35]

It is generally the duty of a Basque who has been successful or at least established a place for himself in the United States, to send over for members of his family to join him. Thus, someone who has established a sheep ranch, will often call over his brothers and sisters to assist him in the enterprise. In one such case, a Basque, who had been about middle-way in terms of his age in his family, was called to the United States to take over his older brother's sheep ranch. When the elder brother died, the younger inherited the entire ranch. Today, with most of his older brothers and sisters deceased, he is looked upon by his three sisters in the United States, as being the etxe jauna, both because he brought them over from Spain and because he is now the eldest surviving member of the family.

It has been said that:

> Pour être un Basque authentique, trois choses sont requisés: porter un nom sonnant qui dise l'origine; parler la langue des fils d'Aïtor, et ... avoir un oncle en Amérique. (Lhande, xvii).

Because of this, researchers in the Basque Country can scarcely study the Basques without taking into account this emigration along kin lines. By "Amérique," of course, is meant the whole of the New World.

It is not unusual, as noted in Chapter I of Part II, for a Basque not to correspond with his home family for many years. This would most often occur if the immigrant were not able to bring over other relatives.

Even if immigration is seen as "temporary," there is a tendency to send immigrants along kin lines. A young Basque boy was interested in pursuing a career in electrical engineering outside of Spain. He thought of going to England. His mother, feeling that England was too "loose moraled" made the boy go to San Francisco to live with his uncle. Though the uncle runs a Basque hotel directly on San Francisco's Broadway (the home of topless clubs), his mother feels he is safe simply because he is with his uncle.

Those Basques who have become successful in sheep ranching will often bring over other Basques from their own home province. So, "men originally for Navarre would usually apply [to have sent] for a man from their native province (Nason, 42)." More of this will be presented in Chapter V of this part.

CHAPTER IV

BASQUE TOKORO-MON

This phenomenon, for the Basques, is closely allied with much of the material presented above. Upon first contact, most Basque-Americans will reply that "we are all Basques," and attempt to minimize the differences between French and Spanish Basques or between the various provinces within these divisions. But these differences become more apparent with time and tend, in broad terms of preferred associations, to coalese along home-associated lines.

This is clearly the case in the tri-partite division of Western Basque settlements, though certainly historical factors may account for this.

These differences between provinces and even between towns are a common feature of Basque life in Europe and it is not likely that they fail to occur among first generation Basque-Americans. The second and third generation tend to lose these feelings as well as the degree of other "ethnic" characteristics. But, some feelings do exist of tokoro-mon as is the case of a second generation Basque lawyer who often jokes that the people from his father's village are the "best Basques" in the territory and are the most successful.

In my experience, the systems of associations established along tokoro-mon lines are not nearly so structured as those among the Japanese reported in Part I. In the broadest sense, Basque tend to prefer to associate with other Basques. This was especially true in their earlier experience in the United States (Edlefsen, 1949). In terms of hiring, Basques in Idaho will often speak of "white" boys (non-Basques) and "Basque boys" (Basque-Americans). In talking with Tasques particularly of this area a feeling of preference for Basque associations still appears to exist. It is not nearly so pronounced in other areas, where Basques are more clearly in the minority. As noted above, the hiring of Basques from the old country often went along home-based associational lines, though this was not always consistently the case. Reasons for such deviations are obscure.

For the Basques, it would have to be said that there is a tendency for tokoro-mon type relations to exist, but not a certainty. Aside from their diligence and the intensity of their application to their occupations, their ability to get along with members of the dominant culture has assisted them in their adaptation to the United States. While some enclavement tendencies were noted for early Basque immigrants, this is not the case today, except, perhaps, in small towns. Associations among second and third generation Basques almost lack completely this tendency. The evidence for tokoro-mon among the Basques, then, is not as complete in my data as I, for the purposes of my theory, would like it to be. The tendency, however, is certainly there, though not well developed.

CHAPTER V

THE ROLE OF INSTITUTIONAL PATHWAYS

Generally speaking, the Basques have been very adept at organizing institutional pathways to assist themselves and their fellow Basques in adapting to American life.

Basque Hotels

In almost every area in which there are Basques, one will find "Basque bars," where local Basques gather to talk over old times both in America and in the Basque country. Often, these bars will be connected with boarding houses of "Basque hotels," which serve meals both to their Basque borders and to non-Basque members of the community. Some writers have felt that Basque boarding houses especially have been responsible for the short-lived early enclavement of the Basques (Edlefsen, Gaiser) but I do not feel that this is necessarily the case. More than one informant has reported that upon his arrival in the West, he proceeded to the local Basque boarding house to find someone who could speak his language. It was a place where the immigrant could find help and job information, especially in the early days when Basque immigration was not as closely tied to occupation as it later became.

The distribution of these "hotels" (more along the lines of the European pension or boardinghouse) meshes with the distribution of the larger Basque communities. Some of the larger areas, such as Boise, may only be able to count one or two of these establishments remaining today, while smaller areas still are able to maintain as many as Gardnerville-Minden, Nevada, with its five![36]

There are those Basques who would remain in the hotels and not venture into the surrounding community and these persons generally returned to the Basque country to stay, having been little touched by American customs and speaking hardly any English (Douglass, 1968). Those who did decide to become residents tended to move early from them and to establish themselves in the community at large.

The idea that these boarding houses represented a "bit of the Basque country transported to the United States" is not entirely true. One young man, who is in San Francisco studying electrical engineering, reports that while the food served in the Basque hotel in which he lives is similar to Basque cooking, it is not the same and, he feels, not intended to be the same. The principle purpose of the boarding house appears to be that of providing a meeting ground for the Basques-- both to meet among themselves and to meet with prospective employers. Today, those Basques still coming to this country as sheepherders will often go to them during their vacations in order to save money.[37]

The exact role of these boarding houses and their history has been looked into, but, as yet, not fully reported.

Basque Clubs

Few of the Basque clubs in the United States have actual club houses. The exceptions today are Boise and New York, though the hazards and tribulations of maintaining a "Centro Vasco" are great and the flagging first generation who established them may not be able to keep them going. This, as noted in Part I, is a general pattern for most immigrant groups. Their role in assisting the immigrant in adaptation in the past was great, however.

Probably one of the most active was the Boise Centro Vasco. Its purpose was clear and its statement of purpose coincides with the most complete of the voluntary associations reported for other groups.

> The American-Basque Fraternity is a corporation organized to encourage, foster, and promote the Americanization of its members, by aiding and assisting those who are not naturalized citizens of the United States to familiarize themselves with its constitution and laws and become citizens thereof, to provide facilities for and encourage the learning and use of the English language. To deliver financial aid and assistance to its members. ... To encourage, foster, conduct, and hold games of handball, golf, lawn tennis, and all classes of athletic amusements and sports, indoor and outdoors, also to provide for the pleasure, exercise, recreation and entertainment of its members. To erect, maintain, and operate club houses and libraries for the purpose of holding its meetings, conducting games, and entertainments for the education, pleasure, recreation and social relation and friendship among its members. (Anduiza)

The economic assistance provided by the Basque clubs in the United States has been termed by one Basque as "an early form of Social Security."

Unemployment benefits, sickness insurance, bural plans and so on were provided through the Basque clubs. Not all Basque clubs provide such a full range of services, but most adhere to the idea of both helping the immigrant to adapt and giving him tokoro-mon based horizontal association ties. Clubs exist in most of the Basque areas and vary in the number of times they meet and the services they provide.

The New York Centro Vasco holds picnics during the year and a yearly "Aberri Eguna" celebration, at which time it issues a program containing advertising and information about Basques in the United States. Newly organized clubs exist in Reno, Nevada and Grand Junction, Colorado. Clubs also are found in Buffalo, Wyoming, San Francisco, Ontario, Oregon and there is also a Southern California Eskualdunak Club, centering around La Puente. Small clubs also exist, but meet less frequently and offer fewer services in Ely, Winnemucca, and Elko, Nevada and in Redwood City, California. A more complete detailing of these including some speculations on their interconnections and origins is found elsewhere (McCall, 1967).

Many of these clubs have dance groups for their members. Some, such as the Oinkari of the Boise Club, have travelled extensively throughout the United States, but others equally interested are found in Ely, Nevada and the San Francisco group even has its own txistulari.[38] The New York Club has a dance group as well.

Membership qualifications for most of these are either being of Basque descent or being married to a person of Basque descent. Again, as with the case of other group's voluntary associations, not all of the Basques in the United States belong to these voluntary associations.

As yet, these clubs have remained relatively isolated from each other[39] and even some animosity, reminiscent of the village loyalties of the Old Country, often occurs among them. At one Basque club, third generation members, in connection with their dance activities, wanted to learn Basque and a series of classes was led by a local man. Though it is difficult to assess the result of these classes, the teacher of the classes will soon be issuing a method for learning Basque for English speakers resulting from his three years experience in teaching at the Basque Center.[40]

Tokoro-mon and Basque Sheepherding

"Surely no other group [in the United States] has received so much specific attention and legislation on the basis of occupational specialization [as the Basques] (Nason, 51)." As was pointed out briefly above, the Basques have been closely tied to the sheep industry since some of their earliest immigration to the United States.

Much has been written about the Basques and the sheep industry in the United States, especially in popular newspaper and magazine articles. Writers tend to divide up along two lines of thought about the Basques and sheepherding: (1) the Basques were accidentally associated with sheep in the United States and many immigrants had never even seen sheep before coming to the American West, and (2) the Basque character is well adapted to sheepherding and it is an occupation he favors. Both views are, of course, extreme and are only true for some immigrants.

I would have to say that the majority of the people I talked to were not very happy with their early years as sheepherders. Young Basques in this country do not enjoy sheepherding, but do it as a means to an end--the chance to earn money and to transfer to other and better occupations. It is a common pattern for a young man to come to this country and, through tokoro-mon ties to become a herder for a few years and then to leave the occupation as soon as possible for better work. This is especially true for French Basques who have never had any sort of immigration restrictions. One study revealed that second generation Basques tended to reject involvement in the sheep industry and favored other occupations (Edlefsen, 1948), while another pointed to the Basques and their descendants tending to monopolize the sheep industry in another area (Gomez-Ibáñez).

Not all Basques come to this country first as sheepherders, though the majority of them probably did in the earlier days of Basque immigration. In San Francisco, a common first job is gardening and there are estimated to be about three hundred Basques working in this trade in the San Francisco Bay Area. In and around Chino, and La Puente, California, immigration is firmly linked with employment in the dairy industry as it has been, incidentally, with Basques going to Argentina for many years. A recent celebration in Tonopah, Nevada pointed up the early Basque participation in mining. Basques were also brought in to herd cattle (McGee).

But, sheepherding remains the main reason for the special importation of Basques into this country. One would suspect that even though transhumance is characteristic of the Pyrenees, there are many Basques who are unfamiliar with herding techniques and who do encounter sheep for the first time in the American West. One student has pointed out how closely American transhumance resembles Pyrenean transhumance and he even makes a case for the Basques being largely responsible for bringing this technique to the West (Gomez-Ibáñez).

In states where sheepherding is important, there has been much agitation for the passing of so-called "sheepherder laws" (Nason) to allow entry to Basques otherwise barred because of the former immigration quotas (Nason). The changes that this system has gone through over the years have strongly affected Basque immigration. In 1965 alone, 1,283 Basques were "imported" by the Western Range Association (originally set up by Basques for Basques). An additional ninety-seven Basques were brought in to Wyoming in that same year by the Basque-run Wyoming Woolgrowers Sheepherders Procurement Program (Gomez-Ibáñez, 23). These "importations" are for restricted temporary employment as discussed above.

Clearly, their occupation, or rather their willingness to take on a particular occupation, has greatly aided their immigration to the United States. It is also very explicit that this immigration takes place along well-defined tokoro-mon lines.

CHAPTER VI

CONSISTENT VALIDATION FOR ADAPTATION

Basque Population and Occupation

The Basques have never represented a sizable amount of the population of this country. Probably the highest estimate of a possible "Basque-American" population of the United States is fifty thousand persons. This, as noted above, would include first, second, and third generation individuals. Also, these persons are not concentrated into one area, though a large concentration may be said to exist in Boise, Idaho, which claims about eight thousand "Basque-Americans." Still, the United States has never felt that it was being threatened by a flood of Basque immigrants. One might almost say that the Basques "slipped into" the United States and except for occasional mentions are not generally known to even exist in the numbers that they do.[41]

For the most part, the Basques have taken occupations which, for the early phase of their individual immigration, were mainly unskilled labor jobs. As noted above, they have worked as sheepmen, gardeners, miners, ranch hands of various types, and so on. But, again owing to their numbers, they have never threatened other groups with their presence. The only sort of discrimination noted was in Idaho and this was mainly along occupational lines--that is, the traditional "feuding" between cow men and sheep men and was not particularly aimed at the Basques.

A Basque Race?

The Basques, at least for other Basques, do have "racial markers." But these, in the context of American society, are not significant. Except for slightly olive skin and a tendency to dark hair (though this is by no means true in every case), plus some distinctive facial characteristics which Basques usually are aware of, but rarely are noticed by the general population, the Basques have had little difficulty in being a racially "visible" population. In areas where there are a number of Basques, sometimes non-Basques will recognize a Basque on sight, but it is not the usual case. Usually, some added clue, such as beret, will have to be provided. They appear, in all of their various forms, to be "white" and cannot be said to have encountered any difficulty which might be traced to a "racial" origin.

Occupational and Residential Mobility

Enclavement has been noted among the Basques of Idaho, but this was an early and, in my opinion, relatively passing phenomenon. "Basque communities," when people have tried to trace them on city maps, are pretty well non-existent at this point and may never have enjoyed great success. There are a number of reasons for this.

Vertical occupational mobility has always been of great interest to the Basque-American. Entering as he did at a low point on the occupational "ladder" (Gaiser), he would change and continue to rise as quickly as wit, skill, and opportunity would allow. Though there are, I am sure, instances of Basques who have not progressed occupationally, the pattern for the majority is clearly one of upward mobility

(Edlefsen, 1948). Accompanying this upward occupational mobility is, if my theory is correct, an accompanying residential mobility. Since Basques have always exhibited skills and a conscientious desire to keep up their homes, they have never, to my knowledge, been denied access to any community. Therefore, as the individual Basque's income increased, there was a tendency to seek housing on the basis of its monetary value, rather than on the basis of ethnic association. This was the case reported for Boise, Idaho (Edlefsen, 1948; Gaiser; McCullough).

In other areas, Basque neighborhoods have other explanations for their break-up. The majority of the Basque hotels in San Francisco cluster around Broadway below Powell Street, in the old Italian colony of North Beach, just on the edge of Chinatown. Few Basques actually maintain residences there at this time, however, and some of my older informants felt that this was caused by the general break-up of the Basque community following the earthquake in San Francisco in 1906. One informant, born at the corner of Powell and Broadway in 1890 felt that this definitely was the case. She was second generation Basque-American, her grandparents having come to California in 1848. Other informants have noted that shortly before and following the San Francisco earthquake of 1906 many Basque-Americans embarked on a "second migration" to the American Northwest. This finding appears to have been confirmed by other researchers who have discussed the matter with Basques living today in the Northwest (Douglass, 1968).

In fact, for the San Francisco case, the French Basques who make up the majority of the Basque-American population today of about two thousand, are not generally aware of the early Basque settlement in San Francisco. Most of them feel that Basques have only been coming to the Bay Area since the end of World War II or about 1948, which is, in fact, when French Basques first started arriving here in great numbers.

In Bakersfield, a second-generation Basque reported that the community there was disrupted and dispersed by an earthquake in the early 1950's and also by the resettlement of Japanese-Americans in the former Basque area.

There was once an area in Manhattan where most of the Basques of New York City lived, but it was torn down as part of a housing project in 1944 by New York's mayor Al Smith. The Basque center moved out of the area and most of the Basque-Americans dispersed, with many of them moving to Brooklyn,[42] where there is now a neighborhood bar which serves as an informal meeting place. The present Basque Center is located in Chinatown and few Basques live near it.

So, the possibility of small enclavements of Basques in the areas in which they have settled has been minimized. Even in an area where they most predominate, Jordan Valley, Oregon, they only constitute about one-third of the population (Gaiser). The diversity of their occupational choices is great (Edlefsen, 1948: 67,70) and is matched by their residential mobility.

Basque Intermarriage

As was mentioned above, in connection with defining who is a Basque and who is not, there has been a great deal of intermarriage between Basques and other Catholic groups, such as the Irish and the Italians. There are even some marriages reported among Protestants, though I cannot give any idea of just how prevalent this tendency might be. One second generation daughter of immigrant parents, who was raised to speak Basque and to know many of the Basque customs, married a non-Basque, non-Catholic whose political affiliation was decidedly different from the surrounding Basque group. The Basques of Idaho tend to be fairly liberal Democrats (Gunther), while her marriage choice is a conservative Republican. When asked why she chose to deviate so strongly from the expectations of her parents and particularly her grandmother, who lives with the family, she said that she thought her college experience had changed her and had predisposed her to making her choice of marriage partner along non-group associative lines. Since Basque-Americans are very keen on education and, fully in the line with the general United States norms, expect their children to attend colleges and universities, I would expect that such changes are likely to occur among the children of the Basque immigrants and their descendants with increasing frequency.

While, in terms of their adaptation, they have exhibited some of the "principle of third generation interest," this does not appear to be a general case for most of the Basque colonies.[43] Interest in being Basque appears to be a passive one, according to one informant. Of course, this cannot be said to be true of all Basques, but certainly many of them. The exact percentages of who feels "more Basque than another" is difficult to estimate.

CHAPTER VII

LANGUAGE DIFFERENCES

The Basques, as noted above, speak a language not firmly related to any other in the world. Many Basques speak Spanish in addition to Basque, particularly because of the anti-Basque language policies of the Spanish central government.[44] And, of course, those who come from the French side often speak French in addition to their Basque. But, there are those who speak only Basque, or at least speak it as a first language and do not do well in either of their adopted languages.

Qyite often it was the case that the child of the immigrant would teach the parents the ways of the community, especially in those areas where the immigrant had little contact with English speakers. Most early Basques exhibited a marked reticence to learning English and many stores in Boise, Idaho and in the smaller towns of Idaho hired second-generation Basques who spoke Basque to wait on immigrant Basque customers. This situation of the children speaking English better than their parents and even serving as advisors to their parents on matters dealing with the larger community was particularly true in the relatively isolated farming areas.

One investigator has felt that in the towns, a situation of trilingualism might exist for Basque-Americans (Gaiser)! That is, that an immigrant might speak English, Spanish, and Basque. The implications of this in terms of considerations of bilingualism (Haugan) have not yet been fully explored.

Many sons and daughters of Basque immigrants recall that they didn't begin to speak English until they entered grade school. A typical story might be:

> The father came to America as a young man, after having worked
> on ships for a number of years. He arrived in Jordan Valley,
> herded sheep, and worked in the mines for a time. He then re-
> turned to Vizcaya, married a childhood friend, and brought her
> back to the New World. In Jordan Valley they reared a family
> of five children. The father now owned a business. In this
> small community, the children went to school and got along well.
> In the home Basque, Spanish, and some English were spoken so
> the children learned the three languages. Few, if any, social
> farness situations developed over the language situation. The
> parents learned English from their children. Minor differences,
> or temporary farness situations arose on matters of discipline
> and home work. The parents encouraged education, and all the
> children eventually left the village to attend college. Two
> daughters are now married, one to a Basque and the other to a
> non-Basque. One daughter has been a secretary to a university
> professor. One son is now a successful businessman, the other
> a rising young lawyer. (Gaiser, 65)

For some, the learning of Basque at home stunted their school careers. Many report that they did not do well in their early grade school years because they did not speak English.

There was always a certain pride the Basque-American felt in being able to speak Basque.[45] There are those among the second and third generation who make a great deal of their knowledge of Basque and will often speak in Basque to immigrant Basques in front of their less knowledgeable Basque-American peers. Sometimes, this habit has irritated those Basque-Americans not knowing Basque. This, of course, is a carry-over from the culture of European Basque.

CONCLUSION

Above I have made an effort to evolve a sequential theory of migration and adaptation, attempting to trace the progress of persons undergoing the similar processes of immigration, urbanization and acculturation. After deriving a seven part theory, I applied this to my own field work among Basque-Americans in the United States, detailing point by point how they exemplified the intentions of my theory.

The questions remaining are: How does this theory work with a wider sample? What effect does the receiving culture have on migration and adaptation, if any? or, Might a similar sequence be necessary to explain the resident group's reaction to the entry of an immigrant group? Is my theory applicable to human migrations throughout history or is it tied to the more recent phenomena of immigrants to America and so-called "Westernization"? My study here has little time depth. I have only been able to superficially consider some of the more in-depth psychological problems of the immigrant, in my sense of the term, and a fuller analysis of immigration on these more intimate terms would be called for.

Certainly, in terms of process, this sequence of events and problems has its relevance to the general theory of socialization and to the larger considerations of man's adaptation in general (Cohen, 1968).

Turning to the Basques in particular, I have only superficially touched upon their activities in this country. I would hope that those interested in more detail would consult the bibliography of materials given after the General Bibliography. I believe that I have demonstrated that the Basques have been successful in their adaptation, in my terms, and further that they will continue to demonstrate, for at least a while, some of their ethnic characteristics. Predictions of when Basque-Americans will cease to be "Basque-Americans"[46] and become "general Americans," are, I believe false speculations based upon an untenable concept--"assimilation."

Assimilation and its analogous term, "amalgamation," smack of the old nineteenth century concept of "the Melting Pot." Considerable criticism has already been directed at this process (Glazer and Moynihan). So prevalent, however, is this idea of everyone in the United States becoming a faceless and "identity-less" being, that it leads even recent writers to make predictions about when this immigrant group or that immigrant group will "blend" with the "general population."

I strongly question, and this is an important point for immigrant studies in general, the idea that there is a dominant "American" personality except in the most broad terms. I have mentioned this above in greater detail.

One example from the Basque-American research will illustrate my point. One writer predicted that "by 1950, [the Basques] will have closed their Basque culture book and have largely merged with the surrounding groups (Gaiser, 188)." This statement was written in 1944 and from his view, it may have seemed that this might come to pass. However, possibly the greatest activity among the Basque-American community has been from the late nineteen fifties until the present time with the founding of a plethora of Basque clubs and dance groups.

I do not feel that it is meaningful for me to speak about "assimilation" and that is why I have chosen to speak of adaptation. "Adaptation" implies only that

51

the group in question is able to co-exist amicably with other groups around it and
has no implications for cultural homogeneity.

FOOTNOTES

1. Herskovits quotes from the Cuban scholar, F. Ortiz a definition of "transculturation." The term, widely used by South American sociologists, has not found much favor among American students, though it has been in the literature since 1940. The term attempts to convey the interactional aspect for two cultures meeting, rather than the more one sided appearing term, "acculturation" (Herskovits, 173).

2. The idea that cities and the countryside represent different environments may be best credited to Robert Redfield. It is beyond the scope of this thesis to examine the nature of this "folk-urban construct" as proposed by him. The literature criticizing, from many points of view, his theoretical concept has been reviewed elsewhere (Allison). My own view, briefly, is that cities represent clusterings of neighborhoods and that the anomie noted so often to characterize the world view of the urban dweller is probably more a phenomenon of the unsupported immigrant than a long time urban dweller. This view of cities has been noted by other investigators of urbanization (Abu-Lughod). Articles describing a so-called "urban world view" in a peasant setting (Reina) exemplify the confusion which may result from a rigid interpretation of Redfield's construct. The peasant society is not harmonious and the city is not wholly impersonal, but they are different, if only when one considers the numbers of persons involved.

3. A more complete rationale for using adaptation instead of the more usual term, "assimilation," is at the end of Part II.

4. The idea of peoples of diverse cultural origin being "blended" into a harmonious whole is part and parcel of what I have mentioned just above with respect to the concept of "assimilation." Modern nation building in Africa often requires that such a concept be perpetuated so as to justify even the formation of a political entity. Note the difficulties along tribal lines of Nigeria. The problem of controlling heterogeneous cultures and attempting to have them work together is not unique to so-called "new" nations, but is also a difficulty faced by European states. Spain is not unified because of problems of culture, for example. France and the United Kingdom also have noticable minorities who resist being identified with the larger "national" group.

5. The Social Science Research Council Summer Seminar on Acculturation, hereafter to be referenced simply as "Social Science Council" was held in the middle part of the last decade in the hope that some sort of direction and theoretical unity might be evolved regarding acculturation and related phenomena. Participants in the Seminar were three anthropologists (Bernard J. Siegal, Evon Z. Vogt, James B. Watson) and one sociologist (Leonard Broom). A fourth anthropologist, Homer G. Barnett, participated in the Seminar, but apparently did not participate in the writing of the summary and his view of the proceedings is appended in a brief note at the end of the larger article.

6. As will be pointed out in the main body of the thesis, this sequential theory (so named because it is expressed in terms of temporally related concepts) is mainly concerned with the immigrant--the first generation, as I will refer to them from time to time. The breakdown of "ethnic" or immigrant ties occurs almost always among the children of the immigrants. By "breakdown," I am

referring to the practicing of certain customs identifiable as having origi-
nated in the immigrant's place of origin ceasing to be continued as well as
the equally important disintegration of associational preferences along solely
home-based (which may or may not be "ethnic" for the purposes of my theory)
ties. For some of the groups mentioned, I will show that adaptation does not
occur even in second generation individuals and that is why I have separated
the two processes of "migration (the actual transplanting process)" and
"adaptation (the efforts on the part of the immigrant to get along in his new
environment)."

7. Literature representing other groups will also be referred to at various times
    when relevant, but these sources quoted represent the ones with which I most
    completely dealt.

8. By "preparation," I mean here actual preparatory schooling for adaptation, as
    is supposedly conducted for American Indians on the reservation. Also may be
    included here is the preparation given by the culture to its members who are
    going to emigrate, if this is done c onsciously. More subtle, is the "prepara-
    tion" given by the "compatibility of values" mentioned by Hirabayashi and
    Willard.

9. Voluntary associations will be discussed more fully in a separate section in
    Chapter V, Part II.

10. By "members of his own group," I would mean that the immigrant tends to choose
    his associates by the most home-based tie available to him. If an immigrant
    cannot find a member of his kinship group, he will seek someone from his vil-
    lage, region, "ethnic" group, or even national state. These persons are from
    the "same place," no matter how broadly the immigrant is forced, by the numbers
    available, to define his "same place."

11. This section has also been seen as a series of four points: (1) Voluntary
    associations provide the basis for a new kind of community to take the place
    of the lost one. (2) The basis of their formation is by Tokoro-mon, the limits
    of this "same place" being defined by the available immigrants, from clan to
    nation. (3) They carry out a whole range of community functions. (4) They
    tend to dissolve after the usefulness has expired, usually with the passing of
    the first generation (Anderson, 1968). He also pointed out to me an interesting
    case of Indian immigrants to Mexico City who did not seek to form voluntary
    associations (Butterfield).

12. It is said that "racial markers are arbitrarily assigned and are not determi-
    nants in themselves (Ames, 1968)." This is part of a sociological function of
    "race." Nevertheless, for the purposes of my study, when racial markers are
    visible, it makes it all the easier for a value to be assigned to them. I
    see, then, a corresponding relationship between "racial" visibility and a
    greater tendency for assigning meaning to it.

13. There is considerable bibliography on the problems of the Black Man in the
    United States. I have restricted myself to one source (Glazer and Moynihan),
    even though it contains some imperfections as pointed out above.

14. There is a great deal of literature available on "race," both as a biological
    phenomenon and sociological phenomenon, but it constitutes such a separate and
    complex problem, that I have chosen only to comment on it here.

15. Class differences may also operate here.

16. For the examination which is to follow, I will draw upon my field work described in the Foreword. Separated out from my general bibliography is a special bibliography of sources on Basques in the United States. For the ethnological background to be presented, I draw upon my informants' descriptions of the Basque country and from the available published materials (Caro Baroja, Gallop, Lhande, B. Estornes-Lasa). I have found B. Estornes-Lasa's fourth volume particularly useful since it is a summary of much of the literature on the Basques. Gallop's book remains still the most comprehensive English language source, though Aldape is also of some use. Sources on the Basques have always seemed "obscure" or "lacking" to many American anthropologists. Hopefully, this situation will be remedied by the soon to be published bibliography of Jon Bilbao which is to contain about 150,000 entries (Bilbao, 1968). If this bibliography is published by the University of Nevada Press, in connection with that University's Basque Studies Program, it would be all the better. It is intended now for publication by Editorial Auñamendi (San Sebastian, Spain) as part of their comprehensive "Encyclopaedia of Basque Culture."

17. The first thesis I list in my bibliography was actually concerned with "The Spanish Element," though much of her material is about the Basques in Nevada (Becaas).

18. In addition to the sources I quote above, I have also used Kemnitzer (1963) as a guide to organization. I might also note that I have only occasionally given citations in Chapter I. Also, I have rarely cited informants opinions and I often make statements about Basque-Americans without a source. I have done this because, based upon my bibliographic research and my field data, I feel that the expression of my opinion represents a valid assertion. When I am speculating and do not have corroborative data, I note that. I have also consulted with other students of Basque life in the United States. Professor Guillermo Céspedes, of the Department of History of the State University of New York at Stony Brook, is now researching early Basque-American history. Dr. Morton Levine intends to promote Basque research in the United States and Europe with an institute along the lines of Nevada's Basque Studies Program. James Kelly is just now completing at Harvard University a senior thesis on Basque entrepreneurship. Father Juan P. Maguna, in the Anthropology Department of New York University in New York City, intends to write a Master's thesis on Basques in Idaho. A second-generation Basque, Frank Araujo, of the Anthropology Department of the University of California at Davis has tentative plans for studying bi-lingualism among Basques in California. But these plans may change. Another second-generation Basque, Angie Berry, intends to write a Master's thesis on European Basque folklore for the Folklore Program of the University of California at Berkeley, under Dr. Alan Dundes. Jose Elgorriaga, Assistant Professor of Foreign Languages at Fresno State College, is also a second-generation Basque and has indicated to me his interest in studying the Basques in California. Other American scholars have also shown an interest in Basque research as the files of the Basque Studies Program will reveal.

19. Much bibliography exists, especially on Basques in Latin American countries. Basques in Mexico City (Iglesia, Peza), Venezuela (J. Estornes-Lasa, Royas, Gonzalo Salas, Ponte), Uruguay (Collier, Ortagul), Chile (Fernandez-Pradel), Columbia (Parsons) and Argentina (G arciarena, Guaresti, Deffontaines, Moch, Garaico Echea) have published sources. Details regarding the role in the

"discovery" and settling of Latin America are numerous (Ispizua, Xamurre, M. Estornes-Lasa, Ortiz y San Pelayo, Beltran y Fozipide, Bilbao). Periodicals on Basque affairs are printed in Mexico City (Euzko-Deya), Buenos Aires (Euzko-Deya) and Caracas (Gudari). I have found no sources on Basques in Australia, though there appears to be a "Basque Society Gure Txoko" in Melbourne and News of Australian Basques is found in a regular column of the Boletin Informativo del Banco de Vizcaya. I found no mention of Basques in the Philippines, but I do know that a "Guernica Restaurant" in Manilla has a subscription to Mexico City's Euzko-Deya. In Paris there is a plan to publish an international directory of Basques and their descendants called "Nor/Nun." The publisher is a M. Dardy. Basques appear to be the most numerous in Venezuela and Argentina. Large Basque Centers are found in both countries and an "Instituto Americano de Estudios Vascos" exists in Buenos Aires and has produced a "Boletin" for about twenty years.

20. While many think of the Basques solely in terms of their mountain village peasant life, it is well to remember that the present-day Basque country in Spain is one of the most heavily industrialized parts of Spain, with the large urban centers of Bilbao and San Sebastian. The French Basque country is much more rural and is one of the least industrialized parts of France. These differences are often obscured and convey a mistaken impression of the Basque country to the outsider. My description is concerned only with rural Basques.

21. Transhumance is the seasonal shifting of herded livestock (sheep, for the Basques) for pasturage.

22. See Figure 1.

23. A common proverb reflecting this close tie of the Basques to the church is, "Qui dit Basque, dit Catholique."

24. This is a part of the ritual harassment for divorcees who remarry, as well as for the breaching of other community codes. The charivarri is never used to enforce the civil codes imposed by the Spanish and French central governments, but only "Basque law."

25. Martha Cook, a second-generation Basque living in San Francisco intends to study the survival of this custom among United States Basques for her Master's thesis in Anthropology at San Francisco State College.

26. Serological analysis is often very useful for determining population homogeneity. Also, it might be noted that the high Rh negative factor among females could effectively prevent the production of children from non-Basque Rh positive spouses.

27. See Aranzadi.

28. I have compiled a bibliography which has been submitted to the Boletin del Instituto Americano de Estudios Vascos, for publication in 1968.

29. There are a number of different "American character traits." These traits given here are supposed to be representative of the "American middle class," and are used more for their heuristic value than as a precise representation of "American character."

30. My examination draws heavily on Leonard Kasdan's work which, in turn, was based on Hagan's and Parsons' work in Columbia.

31. There is a great deal in the psychological literature on the problems of the "first born."

32. It is not surprising that Basques who have their fortunes in the United States find difficulty in returning to Basque life. They learned to be adults in the United States, since most Basque males emigrate in their late teens. It would be interesting to compare retournees from Latin America with those from the United States to see which were better able to return to their home villages after having spent some time away.

33. Informally, though in no printed source I am aware of, it has been reported to me that there is a high rate of chronic alcoholism and suicide in the Basque country.

34. A very tasty Basque sausage, very different from the Mexican or Portugese kind.

35. There is a problem in defining just what is a Basque in the American context. Merely having a Basque last name does not assure "Basqueness." "Basques," for American Basques may also have non-Basque names. Generally, for purposes of membership in Basque clubs one must have at least one parent who is Basque and carries a Basque name. With this criteria, there are said to be about fifty thousand "Basques" and their descendants in the United States. There are no published sources that can either confirm or deny this with any sort of definite proof.

36. A survey of "Basque hotels" was made by Tom Frye, when he was in the Department of Anthropology at the University of California at Berkeley. So far as I know, the only paper to result from his work is a small bibliography on the Basques in manuscript form. Alan Dundes, of Berkeley, showed me the copy he has in his possession.

37. With the loosening up of immigration quotas, the rigid three-year contract described by Nason has been replaced by a more liberal one.

38. The importance of this unique Basque musician will be detailed in an article to be published in Viltis this summer by me.

39. Father Joseph K. Mallea of the Kempis Residencia in the Bronx, New York hopes to edit a newspaper called Kaixo. The Basque Studies Program would also like to do the same. In the nineteenth century two newspapers were printed for Basques in California--Kaliforniako' Euskal-Herria and the Escualdun Gazeta.

40. Joe Eiguren, of Homedale, Idaho, hopes to print this method himself in the near future. Most methods for learning Basque are in Spanish, with some in French. A course is being organized at the University of Tubingen, in Germany, to teach Basque but I do not know what their text is to be. Eiguren's method is the first designed for English speakers.

41. Some popular movies have appeared about Basques in this country and are listed in the special bibliography under "Miscellaneous."

42. I might note in passing that New York City today has only one Basque restaurant, and that is a recent one. The "Basque hotel" for New York was on Bank Street, over the Valentine Aguirre Travel Agency. The hotel, the restaurant below (the Jai-Alai), and the Agency were all owned by Valentin Aguirre. Aguirre is responsible for having helped a number of Basques to travel to the United States. Today, the agency and hotel are under separate ownership from the restaurant. The hotel is still used as a place to stay in New York by the Basques. How wide the scattering of the New York Basques was in the late 1940's is only a matter for conjecture at this time. It is, however, interesting that Basque connected operations identifying themselves as "Basque" are, I am told, found scattered about the Eastern United States. Two Basque restaurants are in Cambridge, Massachusetts. One is owned by a French Basque, Chez Jean, and the other by an apparently nationalistic Spanish Basque, who uses the old Basque name for Pamplona, Iruña, for the name of his restaurant. Though I have little background information on it, I do know that a liquer called "Amer-Basque" is manufactured in Detroit, Michigan.

43. The dance groups are always a popular way of attracting young people to an ethnic group. I must remain somewhat divided within myself as whehter or not this "principle" exists. On the one hand it would appear that it does, what with the recent activity of Basque clubs and celebrations, such as the ones in Ely and Elko. But, the "Basque community" is made up of first generation Basques all the way to third generation "half-Basques" and who is actually supporting this activity remains obscure. Quite often, too, is the existence of a club or a celebration consisting of a large number of participants who are merely "spectators" who do not involve themselves in the hard work of planning. In this way, a Basque club may have a sizable membership list, but the burden of running the group may fall upon less than a dozen persons and possibly even less.

44. Until fairly recently, the Basque language was forbidden in print and to be spoken by the Spanish central government. This is closely connected with the efforts of the various Basque nationalist groups who have been active since the Spanish Civil War. Some have the opinion that Basque nationalism is dying ("The New Basques") or that Basque nationalism is purely a Spanish Basque phenomenon (Irola). However, recent reports from the Basque country would appear to indicate that this is not the case (Szulc, 1967a, 1967b, 1968). Published sources are available. Periodicals such as Alderdi, Embata, and Gudari are totally political in their content, while the Euskal-Deya magazines printed in Mexico City and Buenos Aires contain both political and items of cultural interest. OPE (Oficina Prensa Euzkadi) has been released daily for a number of years from the Paris office of the Basque Government in Exile and provides an excellent chronicle of the movement. Large archives exist in Paris and in the Centro Vasco of Caracas, Venezuela. Basque nationalists have dispersed to many parts of the world and some even went to Russia (Dolores Ibarruri, "La Passionaria"). This complex movement has not, to my knowledge, been fully explored in a recent work. It is not, of course, unrelated to other movements for statehood of other minorities, such as the Ukrainians, Welch, Catalans, Tyroleans, or Bretons. But, unlike these and other groups, the Basques are the only ones who can lay claim to a complete separateness from the national group with whom they live at present (Olano). It would certainly be well worth any historian's time to explore the history of the Basque nationalist movements from their inception in the late nineteenth century with Sabino de Arana Goiri to the present time. Aside from any value the movement

may have in and of itself, its detailed and objective recounting would make a most valuable addition to the literature of political science, international relations, or history and ought to be studied.

45. An area demanding investigation for anthropologists, anthropologically oriented linguists and psycholinguists is a possible connection between speaking an "ethnically related" language and individual in-group identity. For the Basques, this appears to be particularly true. At the very base of it, Euskaldunak ("Basque person") means "one who has the language." "The language," of course refers to Euzker or Basque. A Basque who does not speak Basque, I feel, suffers identity problems. This may often lead to a compulsive dedication to studying or collecting "things Basque." Basques who do not natively speak Basque will often go to great lengths to learn it. One industrialist in Mexico City, in an effort to learn Basque, has allowed only Basque to be spoken in his household.

46. The term "Basque-Americans" indicates their "transcultural" (Ortiz) state-- their mixture of "Basque" and "American" traits. This does not mean that when I refer to "Poles in America" or "Italians in America," that they are any less "American" than the Basques or other foreign born American citizens. My use of the term "Basque-American" means first, second, third, and even fourth generation individuals. Being designated a "Basque-American" is a classifica- tion that is both bestowed by the Basque-American community and chosen by the individual who wishes to be so affiliated. Perhaps the formation of "ethnic groups" and their attendant social clubs in second and third generations func- tions as some sort of identity validators, such as millenarian or nativistic movements have been described to do (Wallace, 34-38).

ABLON, Joan
1964   Relocated American Indians in the San Francisco Area.   Human
Organization 23:296-304.

ABU-LUGHOLD, Janet
1967   Migrant Adjustment to City Life: The Egyptian Case. In Peasant
society: a reader. Jack M. Potter, May N. Diaz and George M. Foster, eds.
Boston, Mass., Little, Brown and Company.   384-398.

AGUIRRE y LECUBE, Jose Antonio De
1944   De Guernica a Nueva York pasando por Berlin.   Buenos Aires,
Editorial Vasca EKIN.

ALBERDI, F. and others
1958   The blood groups of the Spanish Basques.   Journal Royal Anthropological
Institute 87, pt. 2:217-221.

ALDAPE, Ignacio
1963   The Basque Country. Barcelona, Editoral Noguer.

ALLISON, John Victor
1967   Robert Redfield's folk-urban construct. Unpublished Master's thesis,
San Francisco State College.

AMES, David
1968   Personal communication.

ANDERSON, Robert T.
1966   Rotating credit associations in India. Economic Development and
Cultural Change 16:334-339.

ANDERSON, Robert T. and Barbara Gallatin Anderson
1962   Voluntary associations among Ukranians in France. Anthropological
Quarterly 35:158-168.

ARANZADI, Telesforo de
1922   Sintesis métricas de craneos vascos. Revista Internacional de
Estudios Vascos 10:1-60.

ASTILARRA
n.d.   Historica documental de la guerra en Euzkadi. Mexico City, Editorial
Vasca.

ATKINSON, John W. and Bert F. Hoselitz
1958   Entrepreneurship and personality. Explorations in Entrepreneurial
History 10:107-112.

BARANDIARAN, J.-M. de
1948   Materiales para un estudio del pueblo Vasco: en Ligiñaga (Iaguinge).
Ikuska 6-7:177-184.

BARNETT, Clifford
    1964   Final comments and conclusions. Proceedings of the Rural-Urban
    Conference. Washington, D.C., National Institute of Mental Health. 84-89.

BARRON, Milton L., ed.
    1967   Minorities in a changing world. New York, Alfred A. Knopf.

BARTILSON, T. H.
    1930   Nomads of the western ranges. Travel Magazine 55 (September):23-25,
    46.

BEALS, Ralph L.
    1951   Urbanism, urbanization, and acculturation. The American Anthropologist
    53:1-10.

BELTRAN Y FOZPIDE, R.
    1917   Historia de los vascos en el descrubrimiento, conquista y civilization
    de América. (Madrid) Boletin de la Real Academia de la Historia 71:100-105.

BILBAO, Jon
    1958   Vascos en Cuba 1492-1511. Buenos Aires, Ediatorial Vasca EKIN.
    1968   Personal communication.

BILBAO, Juan Manuel
    1946   Basque. In Encyclopaedia of literature. Joseph T. Shipley, ed.
    New York, Philosophical Library. 80-81.

BOWERS, David F., ed.
    1952   Foreign influences on American life. New York, Peter Smith.

BROOM, Leonard and John I. Kitsuse
    1955   The validation of acculturation: A condition to ethnic assimilation.
    American Anthropologist 57:44-48.

BROPHY, William A. and Sophie Aberle
    1966   The Indian: America's unfinished business. Norman, Oklahoma,
    University of Oklahoma Press.

BROWN, James S., Harry K. Schwarzweller and Joseph J. Mangalam
    1963   Kentucky Mountain migration and the stem family: An American varia-
    tion on a theme by LePlay. Rural Sociology 28:48-69.

BRUNER, E. M.
    1956   Primary group experience and the process of acculturation. American
    Anthropologist 58:605-623.
    1961   Urbanization and ethnic identity. American Anthropologist 63:508-521.

BUTTERWORTH, D. S.
    1962   A study of the urbanization process among Mixtec migrants from
    Tilaltongo in Mexico City. América Inoigena 22:257-274.

CARO BAROJA, Julio
    1944   La vida rural de Bidasoa (Navarra). Biblioteca de Tradiciones
    Populares. Madrid, Conselo Superior de Investigationes Cientificas, Instituto
    de Nebrija.

1958   Los Vascos. Madrid, Ediciones Minotauro.

CAUDILL, William and George DeVos
  1956   Achievement, culture and personality: the case of the Japanese-
  Americans. American Anthropologist 58:1102-1126.

CAVAN, Sherri Eileen Cage
  1966   Liquor license: An ethnography of bar behavior. Chicago, Illinois,
  Aldine Publishing Company.

CHALLET, Father P.
  1967   Personal communication.

CHALMERS, J. N. Marshall, Elizabeth W. Ikin and A. E. Mourant
  1949   The ABO, MN and Rh blood groups of the Basque people. American
  Journal Physical Anthropology No. 7:529-544.

CHANCE, Norman A.
  1963   Acculturation, self-identification and personality adjustment.
  American Anthropologist 67:372-393.

COHEN, Yaheudi A., ed.
  1966   Social structure and personality: a casebook. New York, Holt,
  Rinehart and Winston.
  1968   Man in adaptation. The cultural present. Chicago, Aldine Publishing
  Company.

COLLIER, Barnard L.
  1967   In Punta del Este, a Basque tavern. New York Times March 13:43.

COOK, Martha
  1967   Personal communication.

COON, Carlton S. and Edward E. Hunt, Jr.
  1965   The living races of man. New York, Alfred A. Knopf.

COWGILL, Donald O.
  1961   Value assumptions in recent research on migration. Sociological
  Quarterly 2:263-280.

CREET, Roger Anthony Patrick
  1967   The Lebanese stranger-enclave in West Africa: a study of migration,
  family organization and economic life. Unpublished Master's thesis, San
  Francisco State College.

DARDY, Andre L., ed.
  1968   Nor-Nun: Dictionnaire biographique des Basques, Basques d'honneur
  et amis des Basques. Paris, Annuaire Mondial des Basques.

DE VOS, George and Hiroshi Wagatsuma
  1967   Japan's invisible race. Caste in culture and personality. Berkeley
  and Los Angeles, University of California Press.

DEFFONTAINES, Pierre
1952   Participation des Pyrenees au peuplement des Pays de la Plata.
Zaragoza, Primer Congreso International del Pirineo del Instituto de Estudios
Pirenaicos.

DOUGLASS, William
1966   Death in Murelaga. Unpublished Master's thesis, University of Chicago.
1967   Choice making in two Spanish Basque villages. Unpublished Ph.D.
dissertation, University of Chicago.
1968   Personal communication.

EDITOR
1956   This issue and others. American Anthropologist 56:972,1166.

EMBREE, J. F.
1939   New and local kin groups among the Japanese farmers of Kona, Hawaii.
American Anthropologist 41:400-407.

ESTOURNES LASA, Bernal
1967   Orígenes de los Vascos. San Sebastian, Spain, Editorial Auñamendi.
IV vols.

ESTORNES LASA, J.
1948   La compania guipuzcoana de Carácas. Buenos Aires, Editorial Vasca
EKIN.

ESTORNES LASA, Mariano
1961   Gentes Vascas en America. San Sebastian, Spain, Editorial Auñamendi.

ETCHEVERRY, M. A.
1947   El factor rhesus en personas de ascendencia ibérica residentes en la
Argentina. Semana Médica November 25.
1949   Grupo sanguineo y factor Rh en los Vascos. Revista de la Sociedad
Argentina de Hematologia Hemoterogia No. 1:114-118.
1959   Grupos sanguineros y el factor Rh en los Vascos. In La raza Vasca,
Telesforo Aranzadi Jose Miguel Barandiaran, Miguel Angel Etcheverry. Zarauz,
Spain, Editorial Icharopena.

FERNANDEZ-PRADEL, Pedro Xavier
1930   Linajes vascos y montañeses en Chile. Santiago, Chile. Santiago,
Chile, Centro Vasco.

FORSTER, Walter O.
1965   The immigrant and the American national idea. In In the trek of the
immigrants, O. Fritiof Ander, ed. Rock Island, Illinois, Augustana College
Library. 157-178.

FRIEDL, Ernestine
1964   Greek peasants in Athens. Proceedings of the Rural-Urban Migration
Conference. Washington, D.C., National Institute of Mental Health. 57-62.

GALINDEZ, Jesus de
1947   El derecho vasco. Buenos Aires, Editorial Vasca EKIN.
1957   La tierra de Ayala y su fuero. Burenos Aires, Editorial Vasca EKIN.

GANS, Herbert
    1966   Urban villagers. New York, The Free Press.

GAISER, Harold
    1966   Personal communication.

GALLOP, Rodney
    1930   A book of the Basques. London, Macmillan and Company.

GARAICO ECHEA, Abraham Ignacio
    1945   De Vasconia a Buenos Aires; o, La venida de mi madre al Plata
    (historia de una emigracion en el siglo XIX). Buenos Aires, Editorial Vasca
    EKIN.

GARCIARENA, Jose Maria
    1957   Los vascos argentinos frente a la abolicion de los fueros vascos.
    Buenos Aires, Ediciones Alkartasuna de la Federacion de Entidades Vasco
    Argentinas.

GARFINKEL, Harold
    1967   Studies in ethnomethodology. Englewood Cliffs, New Jersey, Prentice-
    Hall, Inc.

GEERTZ, Clifford
    1962   The rotating credit association: A "middle rung" in development.
    Economic Development and Cultural Change 10:243-250.

GINGER, Ray
    1954   Occupational mobility and American life: some historical hypothesis.
    Explorations in Entrepreneurial History 6:234-244.

GLAZER, Nathan and Daniel Patrick Moynihan
    1963   Beyond the melting pot. Cambridge, Mass., M.I.T. Press and Harvard
    University Press.

GONZALO SALAS, Dimon
    1938   Immigracion vasca para Venezuela. Carácas, Impresores Unidos.

GRAVES, Theodore D.
    1965   The opportunity structure in the city and on the reservation by
    Navajo Indian migrants to Denver, Colorado. Navajo Urban Research Relocation
    Research Report, Number 5. Mimeo.
    1967   Acculturation, access and alcohol in a tri-ethnic community.
    American Anthropologist 69:306-321.

GUARESTI, Juan Jose
    1951   Pais vasco y estado espanol; la solucion argentina. Buenos Aires,
    Editorial EKIN.

HAGAN, Everett E.
    1962   On the theory of social change. Homewood, Illinois, The Dorsey Press.

HALPERN, Joel M.
    n.d.   Peasant culture and urbanization in Yugoslavia. Mimeo.

1964   Yugoslavia research. Proceedings of the Rural-Urban Migration Conference. Washington, D.C., National Institute of Mental Health. 49-56.

HANDLIN, Oscar, ed.
    1966   Children of the uprooted. New York, George Braziller.

HANDLIN, Oscar and Mary F. Handlin
    1956   Ethnic factors in social mobility. Explorations in Entrepreneurial History 9:1-7.

HANSEN, Marcus
    1966   The third generation. In Children of the uprooted. Oscar Handlin, ed. New York, George Braziller. 255-271.

HAUGAN, Einar
    1953   The Norwegian language: A study of bilingual behavior. Philadelphia, University of Pennsylvania Press.

HELM, June, ed.
    1967   Essays on the problem of tribe. Proceedings of the 1967 Annual Spring Meeting of American Ethnological Society.

HERSKOVITS, Melville J.
    1967   Cultural dynamics. New York: Alfred A. Knopf.

HIRABAYASHI, James and William Willard
    1964   American Indian migration in the San Francisco Bay Area. Proceedings of the Rural-Urban Migration Conference. Washington, D.C., National Institute of Mental Health. 38-48.

HOGLUND, A. William
    1965   Finnish immigrant farmers in New York, 1910-1960. In In the trek of the immigrants, O. Fritiof Ander, ed. Rock Island, Illinois, Augustana College Library. 141-156.

HORTON, John
    1967   Time and cool people. Trans-action 4 (April):5-12.

HSU, Francis L. K.
    1961   American core value and national character. In Psychological anthropology. Approaches to culture and personality. Homewood, Illinois, Dorsey Press. 209-230.

HUTCHINSON, Edward P.
    1965   A forgotten theory of immigration. In In the trek of the immigrants, O. Fritiof Ander, ed. Rock Island, Illinois, Augustana College Library.

IANNI, Francis A. J.
    1957   Residential and occupational mobility as indices of the acculturation of an ethnic group. Social Forces 36:65-72.

IGA, Mamoru
    1957   The Japanese social structure and the source of mental strains of Japanese immigrants in the United States. Social Forces 35:271-278.

IGLESIA, Emilio Rodriguez
1911   La colonia vascongada en Mexico. Mexico, El eco de Comercio.

IRAOLA, Marion
1967   Basques in France, Letters to the Editor. Fresno Bee. September
19, 16.

ISPIZUA, Segundo de
1914-1919 La historia de los vascos en el descubrimiento, conquista, y
civilizacion de America. Bilbao, Spain, Jose de Lechundi (and others).
VI vols.

JONES, F. Lancaster
1967   Ethnic concentration and assimilation: an Australian case study.
Social Forces 45:412-423.

KASDAN, Leonard
1965   Family structure, migration and the entrepreneur. Comparative
Studies in Society and History 7:345-357.

KELLY, James
1968   Personal communication.

KEMNITZER, Luis S.
1963   Notes on the Basques. Ms.
1964   Urban Dakota kinship and mutual aid systems. Unpublished Master's
thesis, San Francisco State College.

KENNY, Michael
1961a   A Spanish tapestry: town and country in Castille. London, Cohen
and West.
1961b   Twentieth century Spanish expatriates in Cuba: a sub-culture.
Anthropological Quarterly 34:85-93.
1962   Twentieth century Spanish expatriates in Mexico: an urban sub-
culture. Anthropological Quarterly 35:169-180.

KROEBER, A. L. and Clyde Kluckhohm
1963   Culture. A critical review of concepts and definitions. New York,
Vintage Books.

LECUONA, Manuel de
1964   Literatura oral vasca. San Sebastian, Spain, Editorial Aunamendi.

LEWIS, Oscar
1964   Further observations on the folk-urban continum and urbanization
with special reference to Mexico City. Proceedings of the Rural-Urban
Migration Conference. Washington, D.C., National Institute of Mental Health.
1-6.
1966   La vida. New York, Random House.

LHANDE, P.
1910   L'émigration basque. Paris, Nouvelle Librairie Nationale.

LINDBERG, John S.
    1930   The background of Swedish emigration to the United States. Minneapolis,
The University of Minnesota Press.

LITTLE, Kenneth
    1965   The role of voluntary associations in West Africa urbanization. In
Africa. Problems of change and conflict. Pierre L. van den Berghe, ed.
San Francisco, Chandler Publishing Company.

LITWAK, E.
    1960   Geographic mobility and extended family cohesion. American
Sociological Review 25:385-394.

MARIS, Ronald
    1967   Suicide, status and mobility in Chicago. Social Forces 46:246-256.

MARQUER, Paulette
    1963   Contribution a l'étude anthropologique du people Basque et au
probleme de ses origines raciales. Memoire de la Société d'Anthropologie de
Paris.

MARTIN, Harry W.
    1964   Corrolates of adjustment among American Indians in an urban environ-
ment. Human Organization 23:290-295.

MEAD, Margaret
    1943   And keep your powder dry: an anthropologist looks at America. New
York, William Morrow.

MOCH, Andrea
    1909   Del Cantabrico al Plata. Buenos Aires, Tipografica "La Baskonia."

MORANT, G. M.
    1929   A contribution to Basque craniometry. Biometrika 21:67-84.

MOULINIER, Jacques
    1949   The Rh factor in southwestern France. An examination of the Basque
and Bearnais population. American Journal of Physical Anthropology 7:545-548.

MURDOCK, George Peter
    1967   Ethnographic atlas. Pittsburgh, Pennsylvania, University of Pittsburgh
Press.

MYERS, Jerome K.
    1950   Assimilation to the ecological and social systems of a community.
American Sociological Review 15:367-372.

(_____)
    1967   The new Basques. Time Magazine, April 7, 31.

OLANO, Pantaleon Ramirez
    n.d.   Los Vascos no son Españoles. [Carácas, Venezuela] Ediciones Gudari.

ORMOND, P. S.
    1926   The Basques and their county. 2nd ed. London, Simpkin, Marshall,
Hamilton and Kent.

ORTEGA y GASSET, José
    1961   The pride of the Basques. Atlantic Monthly 207 (January):23-25.

ORTIZ, F.
    1947   Cuban counterpoint: tobacco and sugar. New York, Alfred A. Knopf.

ORTIZ Y SAN PELAYO, Felix
    1915   Los Vascos en América. Buenos Aires, Libreria "La Facultad" de
    Juan Roldan.

OTAEGUL, Tomas
    1943   Los Vascos en el Uruguay. Fundacion de Montevideo. Buenos Aires,
    Editorial Vasca EKIN.

PARSONS, James J.
    1949   Antioqueño colonization in western Columbia. Ibero-Americano 32.

PERISTIANY, J. G., ed.
    1966   Honor and shame. The values of a Mediterranean society. Chicago,
    Illinois, The University of Chicago Press.

PETERSEN, William
    1958   A general topology of migration. American Sociological Review
    23:256-266.

PEZA, Juan de Dios
    1956   Leyenda del Colegio de "Las Vizcainas." Mexico City, College of
    Las Vizcainas.

PITT-RIVERS, Julian, ed.
    1963   Mediterranean countrymen. Essays in the social anthropology of the
    Mediterranean. Paris and La Havre, Mouton and Company.

PONS, J.
    1955   Impressiones dermopapetare en Vascos y su relacion con otros
    poblaciones. Barcelona, Trabajos del Instituto (Bernardino de Sahagun) de
    Antropologia y Ethologia 14:57-78.

PONTE, Andres F.
    1946   La puebla de Bolibar. Carácas, Editorial Crisol.

POTTER, Jack M.
    1967   Introduction: peasants in the modern world. In Peasant society:
    a reader. Jack M. Potter, May N. Diaz and George M. Foster, eds. Boston,
    Mass., Little, Brown and Company. 378-384.

QUALEY, Carlton C.
    1965   Immigration, emigration, migration. In In the trek of the immigrants,
    O. Fritiof Ander, ed. Rock Island, Illinois, Augustana College Library. 33-38.

REDFIELD, Robert
    1929   The material culture of Spanish-Indian Mexico. American Anthropologist
    31:602-618.

REINA, Ruben E.
    1964   The urban world view of a tropical forest community in the absence
    of a city, Peten, Guatemala. Human Organization 23:265-277.

RICHARDS, Cara E.
    1963   City taverns. Human Organization 22:260-268.

RIESMAN, David
    1967   Some questions about the study of American national character in the
    twentieth century. In National character in the perspective of the social
    sciences, Don Martindale, ed. The Annals of the American Academy of Political
    and Social Science March, 36-47.

RIQUET, R.
    1962   Les crânes d'Urtiaga en Iziar (Guipuzcoa). Munibe-Revista de ciencia
    naturales Aranzadi.

RIPLEY, William Z.
    1936   The races of Europe. London, Kegan Paul, Trench, Trubner and Company.

ROSEN, Bernard C.
    1967   Race, ethnicity and achievement syndrome. In Minorities in a changing
    world. Milton L. Barron, ed. New York, Alfred A. Knopf. 151-175.

ROYAS, Artisides
    1874   El elemento vasco en la historia de Venezuela. Carácas, Imprenta
    Federal.

SALOUTOS, Theodore
    1964   The Greeks in the United States. Cambridge, Massachusetts, Harvard
    University Press.
    1965   Exodus, U.S.A. In In the trek of the immigrants, O. Fritiof Ander,
    ed. Rock Island, Illinois, Augustana College Library. 197-218.

SCHERMERHORN, R. A.
    1966   The Polish American. In Social structure and personality: a case-
    book. Yaheudi A. Cohen, ed. New York, Holt, Rinehart and Winston. 407-419.

SHEPPERSON, Wilber
    1965   British backtrailers: working class immigrants return. In In the
    trek of the immigrants, O. Fritiof Ander, ed. Rock Island, Illinois, Augustana
    College Library. 179-195.

SOCIAL SCIENCE RESEARCH COUNCIL SUMMER SEMINAR ON ACCULTURATION
    1956   Acculturation: an exploratory formulation. American Anthropologist
    56:973-1002.

SPIRO, Melford E.
    1955   The acculturation of American ethnic groups. American Anthropologist
    57:1240-1252.

SROLE, Leo
    1964   A commentary. Proceedings of the Rural-Urban Migration Conference.
    Washington, D.C., National Institute of Mental Health. 64-68.

STEER, George L.
1963   El arbol de Guernica. Carácas, Venezuela, Ediciones Gudari.

STEWARD, Julian H.
1949   Cultural causality and law: A trial formulation of the development of early civilizations. American Anthropologist 51:1-27.

SWETT, Daniel Henry
1965   Deviant behavior and urban adjustment. Unpublished Master's thesis, San Francisco State College.

SZULC, Tad
1967a   Basque exiles in France still influential in Spain. New York Times. May 1, 22.
1967b   Basque climbers arrested in Spain. New York Times. November 18, 12.
1968   Spanish police seal a city to bar Basque festival. New York Times. April 15, L5.

THOMAS, William J. and Florian Znaniecki
1927   The Polish peasant in Europe and America. New York, Alfred A. Knopf.

TOVAR, Antonio
1957   The Basque language. Philadelphia, University of Pennsylvania Press.

VECOLI, Rudolph J.
1964   "Contadine" in Chicago - a critique of "The Uprooted." Journal of American History 51:404-417.

WALLACE, Anthony F. C.
1966   Religion: an anthropological view. New York, Random House.

WEISENBURGER, Francis P.
1965   A brief history of immigrant groups in Ohio. In In the trek of the immigrants, O. Fritiof Ander, ed. Rock Island, Illinois, Augustana College Library. 81-94.

WINTHER, Oscar Osburn
1965   English migration to the American West, 1865-1900. In In the trek of the immigrants, O. fritiof Ander, ed. Rock Island, Illinois, Augustana College Library. 115-126.

XAMURRE
1966   Colonizadores de la epopeya Americana. Buenos Aires, Editorial Vasca EKIN.

BIBLIOGRAPHY OF MATERIALS RELATING TO BASQUE-AMERICANS

Books or Portions of Books

ADAMIC, Louis
    1945   A Nation of Nations. New York, Harper and Brothers. p. 70.

AUSTIN, Mary
    1906   The Flock. Boston and New York, Houghton, Mifflin and Company.

CALDWELL, Erskine
    1963   Around About America. New York, Farrar, Strauss, and Company.
    pp. 182-193.

CASTILLO PUCHE, Jose Luis
    1963   Oro Blanco. Madrid, Ediciones CID.

CAUGHEY, John Walton
    1954   California. New York, Prentice-Hall. p. 149.

DRAGO, Harry Sinclair
    1924   Following the Grass. New York, The Macauley Company.

EIGUREN, Joe V.
    1964   History and Origin of the Basque. Boise, Idaho, Voter Publishing
    Company.

FAUCHER DE SAINT MAURICE, Narcisse Henri Edouard
    1879   La Canada et les Basques. Trois écrits de M. Faucher de Saint
    Maurice, M. Marmette et M. Le Vasseur. Avant propos du compte de Premio-
    Real. Quebec, A. Côte et Cie.

GACHITEGUY, A.
    1955   Les basques dan l'ouest américain. Bordeaux, Edicion Ezkita.

GREGG, Jacob Ray
    1950   Pioneer Days in Malheur County. Los Angeles, Private printing by
    L. L. Morrison. pp. 213, 301, 407.

GUNTHER, John
    1947   Inside U.S.A. New York, Harper and Brothers. p. 116.
    1951   Inside U.S.A. New York, Harper and Brothers. p. 123.

ISASI, Miriam
    1940   Basque Girl. Glendale, Calif., Griffin-Patterson Publishing Company.

LAXALT, Robert
    1957   Sweet Promised Land. New York, Harper and Brothers.

LOTI, Pierre
    1903   Ramuntcho. Boston, D. C. Heath and Company.

ONTARIO BASQUE CLUB, INC.
    1966   Choice Recipes Compiled by the Ontario, Oregon, Ontario Basque Club.
    Mimeo.

OSSA ECHABURU, Rafael
1963   Pastores y pelotaris vascos en U.S.A. - Impresiones de un viaje a
Norteamerica. Bilbao, Ediciones de la Caja de Ahorros Vizcaina.
1965   Un periodista en vacaciones. Bilbao, La Editorial Vizcaina, S.A.

ROSS, Nancy Wilson
1941   "Among the Basques with a Scotsman," in Farthest Reach. New York,
Alfred A. Knopf. pp. 77-84.

SILIEN, Sol
1917   La historia de los Vascongados en el oueste de los Estados Unidos,
por ... traducciones por Manuel J. de Galvan. New York, Los Novedades, Inc.

TALBERT, Thomas B. (Honorary Editor-in-Chief)
1963   The Historical Volume and Reference Works, Covering Costa Mesa,
Dana Point, Huntington Beach, Laguna Beach, Newport Beach, Orange, San
Clamente, San Juan Capistrano Seal Beach, Villa Park, Westminster. Historical
Publishers, Whittier, California. pp. 96-98.

THOMPSON, Ruth and Chef Louis Hanges
1937   Eating Around San Francisco. San Francisco, Suttonhouse. p. 193.

TINKHAM, H. G.
1929   History of San Joaquin County California with Biographical Sketches.
Los Angeles, Historic Record Company.

YBARRA BERGE, J.
1945   De California a Alaska. Madrid, (_____).

Periodicals and Journals

ALTROCCHI, Julia
1938   The Spanish Basques in California. The Catholic World VCXLVI:417-424.

(_____)
1966   Among the Oldest of Crafts - A New Industry for Idaho and the USA.
Idaho Image April.

(_____)
1963   Annual Basque Festival at Ely, Nevada. Kennevadan Vol. 10, No. 7:
12-13.

ATWATER, Jane
1967   Remember Me - the Lonely One. Frontier Times, August-September:19-21.

(_____)
1937   The Basque Children. The Commonweal Vol. XXVI, No. 8:197-98.

(_____)
1957   Basque Personalities; Basques in the American Melting Pot. Viltis
Vol. XVI (March-April):20.

(_____)
1952   Basque Shepherd. Life May 12:124-9.

BIETER, Pat
  1957   Reluctant Shepherds; the Basques in Idaho. Idaho Yesterdays Vol. 1,
  No. 2:10-15.
  1965   Folklore of the Boise Basques. Western Folklore Vol. 24, No. 4:
  263-270.

BOHN, Frank
  1937   Help the Basque Refugee Children. New Republic Vol. XCI, No. 1176:162.

BRADFORD, Sax
  1942   Sons of the Pyrenees in the Northwest. Travel September:11-15, 32.

BURG, Amos
  1934   A Native Son Rambles in Oregon. National Geographic Vol. LXV, No.
  2:173-235.

COOK, Fred J.
  1966   Who Killed Jesus de Galindez? Fact Vol. 3, No. 2:42-59.

CRESSMAN, L. S. and YTURRI, Anthony
  1938   The Basques in Oregon. The Commonwealth Review Vol. XX, No. 1:367-380.

DAVIS, Miss Eleanor
  1927   The Basques in Malheur County. Commonwealth Review, Vol. IX, No.
  2:51-55.

d'EASUM, Dick
  1963   Euzkaldunak, the Basques of Idaho. Idaho Hunting and Fishing Guide,
  5-8.

DESMOND, Alice Curtis
  1932   Speed Kings of the Pelota Courts. Travel December:19-21, 56.

ECHEVARRIA, Ramon V.
  1963   The Mysterious Basques. Catholic Digest March:140-143.

EDLEFSEN, John B.
  1950   Enclavement Among Southwest Idaho Basques. Social Forces Vol. 29:
  155-158.

E[RQUIAGA], A[lbert]
  1966   Basque Festival in Elko, Nevada. Viltis Vol. XXV (October-November):
  16.

(_____)
  1937   Fate's Hostages: Basque Child Refugees Are Political Football in
  Muddled Washington. Literary Digest June 19:4-5.

(_____)
  1966   General History of Oinkari Basque Dancers. Viltis Vol. XXV (June-
  September):5.

GOYTINO, J. P.
  1889   Kalifornia'ren Ongi Etorria Euskal Erria'ri [Welcome of California to
  Euskal Erria]. Euskal Erria (San Sebastian, Spain) XXI:172-173.

GOYTINO, J. P.
    1889   Sor-lekuaren mina Kalifornian [Homesick in California]. Euskal
    Erria XXI:210-211.

GUTHMAN, Janette
    1945   Basque People of the Northwest. National Wool Grower December.

HARKNESS, Ione B.
    1933   Basque Settlement in Oregon. Oregon Historical Quarterly Vol. 34,
    No. 3:273-275.

(_____)
    1962   High Speed Jai Alai. Sports Illustrated Vol. 16, No. 7:22-27.

HITCHMAN, Sue
    1962   The Constant Beret. Orange County Illustrated Vol. 1, No. 1:40-45.

HUNBELLE, Danielle
    1966   The Basques, the anthropologist's most baffling case. Réalités No.
    192:78-83.

HUNTER, Don L.
    1952   Sound Recording of History. Western Folklore Vol. XI:208-211.

INKSTER, T. H.
    1959   American Basques. American Mercury Vol. LXXXIX, No. 427.
    1960   Basques in America. Contemporary Review (London) Vol. 197:227-229.

KASDAN, L.[eonard]
    1965   Family Structure, Migration, and the Entrepeneur. Comparative
    Studies in Society and History Vol. 7:345-357.

LAXALT, Robert
    1966   Basque Sheepherders, Lonely Sentinels of the American West. National
    Geographic Vol. 129, No. 6:870-888.

LAY, Jr., Beirne
    1947   The Cities of America - Boise. Saturday Evening Post Vol. 219,
    No. 29:22 and 23, 109 and 110.

LEVINE, Morton H.
    1967   The Basques. Natural History LXXVI, No. 4:44-51.

MC CALL, Grant
    1967   The Basques. Viltis December:7-11.

MAGEE, Molly
    1966   A Day on the Mountain with the Basque Buckaroos. Nevada Vol. 26,
    No. 3:4-9, 50-51.

MALLEA OLAETXEA, Joseph K.
    1967   Ameriketako euskaltzaleak - Grant McCall: California-ko gutarra.
    Zeruko Argia (San Sebastian) 22. Ilbeltzak [January 22]. Last page.

(_____)
1960   Our Two Basque Singers Are Off to California for a Month. California Livestock News June 7.

[POST, Annabel]
1960   The Basques in the West. Sunset May:122-127.

READE, John
            The Basques in North America. Royal Canadian Society, Proceedings and Transactions Vol. VI, Sec. 2:21-36.

REID, Alastair
1961   Letter from Euzkadi. The New Yorker Vol. XXXVII, No. 37:171-193.

ROBE, Stanley L.
1953   Basque Tales from Eastern Oregon. Western Folklore Vol. XII:153-157.

ROESCH, Ethel A.
1964   Basques of the Sawtooth Range. Frontier Times Vol. 38, No. 3:14-18.

ROTTIER, Jack
1959   Idaho's Colorful Basques. Scenic Idaho Vol. 12, No. 4:5 and 35.

SCHMITT, Martin
1951   Folklore Sources in the Univ. of Oregon Library. Western Folklore Vol. X:325-328.

SCISCO, L. D.
1924   Precolumbian discovery by Basques. Proceedings and Transactions of the Royal Society of America XVIII:51-61.

SNODGRASS, J. W.
1936   Some California Sheep History. The Pacific Rural Press 132 (September 26):334-335.

(_____)
1952   Spanish Visas for Herders Delayed. The National Wool Grower Vol. 42:6-7.

SPRING, Mary
1957   The Basques. Viltis Vol. XVI (March-April):5-8.
1959   First Western Basque Festival. Viltis Vol. XVII (December):21-24.
1964   The Basque Festival at Elko. Viltis Vol. XVII (December):15-17.

SULLIVAN, Jean
1966   Idaho's Basques, Great Cookery is Part of Their Heritage. The Dodge News Magazine January:20-21.

TAYLOR, Dabney
1964   Christmas in Euzkaldunak. Today's Health Vol. 42 (December):18-19, 72-74.

THANE, Eric
1953   Always He is Alone. Collier's Vol. 132 (July 11) No. 2:40-43.

(_____)
1951   Traditional Festival Ended. Western Folklore Vol. X:177-178.

TURNER, Bill
1967   The Minuteman. Ramparts Vol. 8, No. 7:69-76.

VAN VALKENBURGH, Peter
1924   Shepherd Basques of California. Overland Monthly and Out West
Magazine Vol. LXXXII, No. 8:343-344, 369, 377.

VOEGELIN, C. F. and F. M.
1964   Languages of the World: Native America. Fascicle one. Anthropological Linguistics 6:8-9.

WALLACE, James K.
1950   The Basque Sheepherder and the Shepherd Psalm. Reader's Digest 56
(June):41-44.

WHITE, John M.
1963   Ranchers in the Basque Tradition. New Mexico Magazine Vol. 41, No.
4:30-31, 35.

WILBUR, Terrence H.
1961   The Phonemes of the Basque of Bakersfield, California. Anthropological
Linguistics Vol. 3, No. 8:1-12.

Newspaper Articles

ADAMS, Larry D.
1967   At Last! A Basque Miss Wool. The Fresno [California] Bee California
County Life section September 3:10-F.

ANDERSON, Mike
1960   Basques Note Pioneer Aid Unit Activities. [Boise] Idaho Daily
Statesman April 30.

(_____)
1966   Annual Basque Festival Here July 2nd, 3rd. Elko [Nevada] Daily Free
Press June 25:1.

ANSOLABEHERE, Gracian
1966   The Basques, Central California Register Letters from Our Readers
July 14:3.

(_____)
1962   Basking's Great on Basque Ranch. Salt Lake Tribune February 10.

(_____)
1965   Basque Dancers Display Heritage, Represent Idaho at Fair; Enrich
State in Unique Way. [Boise] Idaho Daily Statesman June 18:14.

(_____)
1936   Basque Dancers Throng Gay Sheepherder's Ball Held Friday Evening,
Capital News [Boise, Idaho] December 19.

(_____)
1967   Basque Days - Lively Events to Draw Crowd, Tonopah [Nevada] Times-Bonanza Friday, July 28:1,5.

(_____)
1966   Basque Fest Highlights Elko Holiday Weekend, Elko [Nevada] Daily Free Press Friday, July 1:1,3.

(_____)
1937   Basque Fraternity Court Battle Gets Under Way, Capital News [Boise, Idaho] April 6.

(_____)
1957   Basque Govt.-in-Exile pres. de Arguirre in N.Y.C. to seek release of de Galindez records; reports all funds de Galindez collected accounted for. New York Times May 11:9.

(_____)
1957   Basque Govt.-in-Exile representative J. Oñatibia seeks to get files and records of Dr. de Galindez, whom he replaced as representative in U.S. after de Galindez vanished; N.Y.S. Pub Admr. contests claim, seeks to have legality of Basque organization established. New York Times April 11:18.

(_____)
1941   Basque Government to Open Office in Boise, Capital News [Boise, Idaho] October 22.

(_____)
1964   Basque Group Due Saturday, The [Winnemucca] Nevada Daily Bulletin Friday, August 7:1.

(_____)
1916   Basque Miners Come to Work in Pennsylvania Fields, New York Times March 30.

(_____)
1938   Basque Names Familiar in Valley With 2,000 Population Estimated, Twin Falls [Idaho] Times March 23.

(_____)
1966   Basque People Whoop it Up at Annual Boise Picnic [Boise] Idaho Daily Statesman August 1.

(_____)
1966   Basque Priest Denies Remarks, Central California Register July 21:2.

(_____)
1966   Basque Professor Sees Berets on Moon by Euzkaldun Bat, Elko [Nevada] Daily Free Press June 30:1.

(_____)
1967   Basque Slate Field Mass, Ely [Nevada] Daily Times July 17:2.

(_____)
1937   Basques Doomed As a Distinct Race; America Impinges, Capital News [Boise, Idaho] July 2.

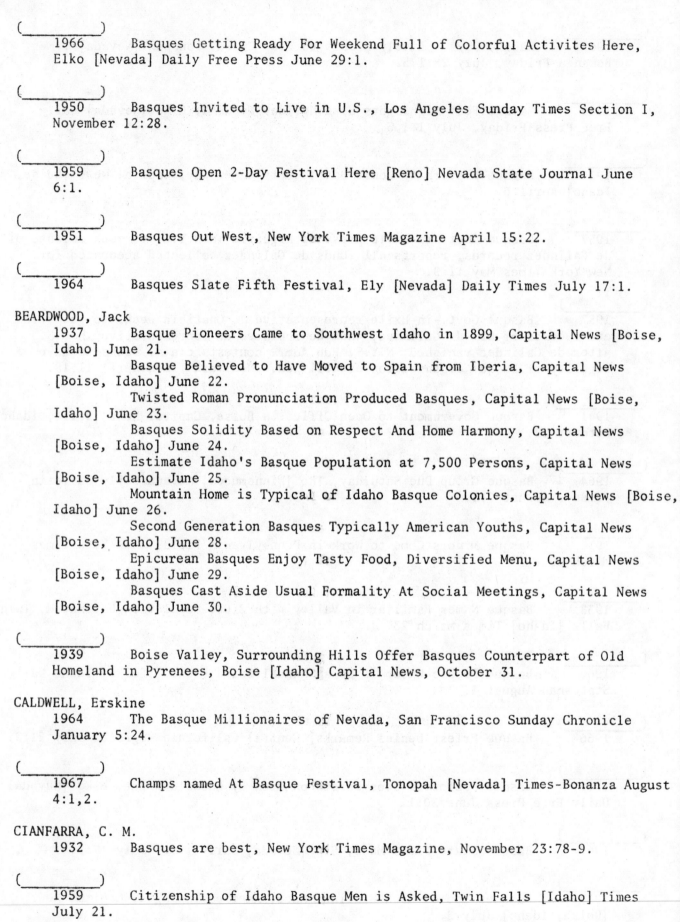

(_____)
1966   Basques Getting Ready For Weekend Full of Colorful Activites Here,
Elko [Nevada] Daily Free Press June 29:1.

(_____)
1950   Basques Invited to Live in U.S., Los Angeles Sunday Times Section I,
November 12:28.

(_____)
1959   Basques Open 2-Day Festival Here [Reno] Nevada State Journal June
6:1.

(_____)
1951   Basques Out West, New York Times Magazine April 15:22.

(_____)
1964   Basques Slate Fifth Festival, Ely [Nevada] Daily Times July 17:1.

BEARDWOOD, Jack
1937   Basque Pioneers Came to Southwest Idaho in 1899, Capital News [Boise,
Idaho] June 21.
            Basque Believed to Have Moved to Spain from Iberia, Capital News
[Boise, Idaho] June 22.
            Twisted Roman Pronunciation Produced Basques, Capital News [Boise,
Idaho] June 23.
            Basques Solidity Based on Respect And Home Harmony, Capital News
[Boise, Idaho] June 24.
            Estimate Idaho's Basque Population at 7,500 Persons, Capital News
[Boise, Idaho] June 25.
            Mountain Home is Typical of Idaho Basque Colonies, Capital News [Boise,
Idaho] June 26.
            Second Generation Basques Typically American Youths, Capital News
[Boise, Idaho] June 28.
            Epicurean Basques Enjoy Tasty Food, Diversified Menu, Capital News
[Boise, Idaho] June 29.
            Basques Cast Aside Usual Formality At Social Meetings, Capital News
[Boise, Idaho] June 30.

(_____)
1939   Boise Valley, Surrounding Hills Offer Basques Counterpart of Old
Homeland in Pyrenees, Boise [Idaho] Capital News, October 31.

CALDWELL, Erskine
1964   The Basque Millionaires of Nevada, San Francisco Sunday Chronicle
January 5:24.

(_____)
1967   Champs named At Basque Festival, Tonopah [Nevada] Times-Bonanza August
4:1,2.

CIANFARRA, C. M.
1932   Basques are best, New York Times Magazine, November 23:78-9.

(_____)
1959   Citizenship of Idaho Basque Men is Asked, Twin Falls [Idaho] Times
July 21.

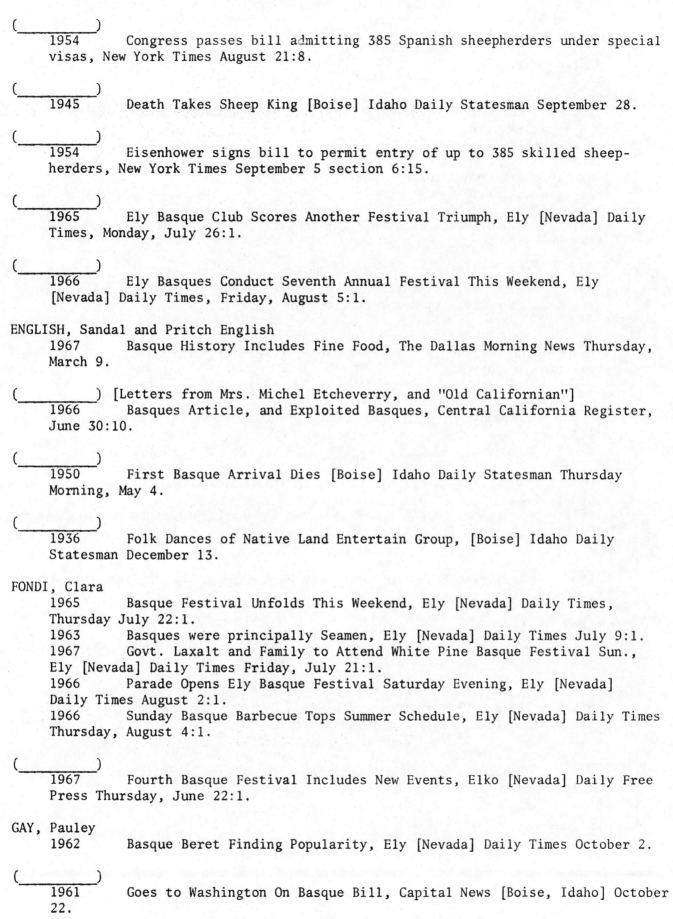

(_____)
1954   Congress passes bill admitting 385 Spanish sheepherders under special
visas, New York Times August 21:8.

(_____)
1945   Death Takes Sheep King [Boise] Idaho Daily Statesman September 28.

(_____)
1954   Eisenhower signs bill to permit entry of up to 385 skilled sheepherders, New York Times September 5 section 6:15.

(_____)
1965   Ely Basque Club Scores Another Festival Triumph, Ely [Nevada] Daily
Times, Monday, July 26:1.

(_____)
1966   Ely Basques Conduct Seventh Annual Festival This Weekend, Ely
[Nevada] Daily Times, Friday, August 5:1.

ENGLISH, Sandal and Pritch English
    1967   Basque History Includes Fine Food, The Dallas Morning News Thursday,
    March 9.

(_____) [Letters from Mrs. Michel Etcheverry, and "Old Californian"]
    1966   Basques Article, and Exploited Basques, Central California Register,
    June 30:10.

(_____)
1950   First Basque Arrival Dies [Boise] Idaho Daily Statesman Thursday
Morning, May 4.

(_____)
1936   Folk Dances of Native Land Entertain Group, [Boise] Idaho Daily
Statesman December 13.

FONDI, Clara
    1965   Basque Festival Unfolds This Weekend, Ely [Nevada] Daily Times,
    Thursday July 22:1.
    1963   Basques were principally Seamen, Ely [Nevada] Daily Times July 9:1.
    1967   Govt. Laxalt and Family to Attend White Pine Basque Festival Sun.,
    Ely [Nevada] Daily Times Friday, July 21:1.
    1966   Parade Opens Ely Basque Festival Saturday Evening, Ely [Nevada]
    Daily Times August 2:1.
    1966   Sunday Basque Barbecue Tops Summer Schedule, Ely [Nevada] Daily Times
    Thursday, August 4:1.

(_____)
1967   Fourth Basque Festival Includes New Events, Elko [Nevada] Daily Free
Press Thursday, June 22:1.

GAY, Pauley
    1962   Basque Beret Finding Popularity, Ely [Nevada] Daily Times October 2.

(_____)
1961   Goes to Washington On Basque Bill, Capital News [Boise, Idaho] October
22.

(_____)
1961   Gold, Not Sheep, Cause Of Idaho Basque Influx [Boise] Idaho Daily
Statesman June 15.

HAYDEN, Carl E.
1960   Bounding Basques, The Salt Lake Tribune Home April 3:4-5.

HELLINGER, Charles
1966   The Long Sheep Trail Through California, San Francisco Sunday
Chronicle and Examiner Punch Section July 3:2.

(_____)
1942   House Grants Basques Right to Stay in U.S., Boise [Idaho] Capital
News February 3.

(_____)
1954   House passes Senate bill to cancel deportation proceedings against
44 Basque sheepherders, New York Times August 19:31.

(_____)
1964   Huge Basque Festival 'A Whopping Success,' Elko [Nevada] Daily Free
Press August 10:1,3.

(_____)
1967   Interest High in Basque Days, Tonopah [Nevada] Times-Bonanza July
21:1.

LANGAN, Jack
1967a   Annual Basque Picnic Coming Up This Sunday, Sheridan [Wyoming] Press
August 11:5.
1967b   Scots May Have St. Andrew's-But The American Basque Has His Annual
Festival, Sheridan [Wyoming] Press September 2:10.

(_____)
1965   Laxalt to Research University Basque Studies Plan, Reno [Nevada]
Evening Gazette August 10:13.

LONGFELLOW, Esther
1941   Picturesque Basque Customs Rapidly Fading From Idaho [Boise] Idaho
Daily Statesman January 27.

MORRISEY, Don
1964   Basque Dances, Ages Old Revived by Boise Troupe For New York Fair
Show [Boise] Idaho Daily Statesman March 22.

(_____)
1967   Music, Dancers and Sports Featured at Basque Festival, Ely [Nevada]
Daily Times July 18:1.

(_____)
1964   National Basque Festival Opens, Elko [Nevada] Daily Free Press August
8:1,3.

NELSON, Dale
    1958   Colorful Basque Customs of 75 Years Ago Are Disappearing to Younger
    Generation's Regret, Lewiston [Idaho] Morning Tribune October 1:8.

(_____)
    1967   1967 Basque Festival Opens, Elko [Nevada] Daily Free Press July 1:1,6.

(_____)
    1936   98-Pound Lamb Auctioned for $315 At Annual Boise Sheepherders' Ball
    [Boise] Idaho Daily Statesman December 19.

(_____)
    1967   Now That Was A Great Festival!, Elko [Nevada] Daily Free Press July
    3:1.

(_____)
    1964   Numerous Activities Highlight Basque Festival, Ely [Nevada] Daily
    Times July 20.

(_____) "O., L."
    1966   Basque-ing in New Glory, An editorial in [Pocatello] Idaho State
    Journal August 17.

OLMOS, Robert
    1966   Old, New Mingle in Tiny Arock, The Oregonian [Portland, Oregon]
    March 6.

(_____)
    1966   Ontario Basque Club Offers Sale of Basque Cookbook, Argus-Observer
    [Ontario, Oregon] August 4:2.

(_____)
    1937   Oregon's Basques: A Friendly, Hard-Working Race, The Oregonian
    [Portland, Oregon] June 20.

PENSON, Betty
    1949   As the Basques Say It- [Boise] Idaho Sunday Statesman May 8.

PETERS, Christie
    1956   Basque Ranchers Dominate West Side Sheep Industry, The Fresno
    [California] Bee Country Life Section September 9.

(_____)
    1947   Picnic, Dance to Mark Basques St. Ignatius Day Observance [Boise]
    Idaho Daily Statesman July 31.

(_____)
    1966   Rancher Leaves Estate Valued at $513,672, The Fresno [California] Bee
    July 22:3-A.

(_____)
    1955   Ranchers to urge bringing in more Basque sheepherders, New York Times
    January 9 section 2:79.

SALINGER, Pierre
    1952   From Pamplona to San Joaquin--Basque Shepherds, San Francisco
    Chronicle June 29:17.
                From Pamplona to San Joaquin--Basque Shepherds, San Francisco
    Chronicle June 30:19.

(_____)
    1956   Senator Lehman protests bills to admit more Basque sheepherders
    while immigration law remains unchanged, New York Times June 21:20.

(_____)
    1966   Seventh Basque Festival Scores Smashing Success, Ely [Nevada]
    Daily Times August 8:1,3.

(_____)
    1967   Sheep Dog Trials Join Basque Festival, Elko [Nevada] Daily Free
    Press June 24:1,6.

(_____)
    1966   A Shepherd From the Hills, Central California Register December
    22:12-B.

(_____)
    1960   Spanish Shepherds Ease Labor Shortage for U.S. Sheepman, Wall Street
    Journal November 29.

(_____)
    1967   The Strength of the Basques Shows in Competitive 'Games,' Elko
    [Nevada] Daily Free Press Monday, July 3:1.

STRENTZ, Herb
    1962   Basques Enrich California Life, The Fresno [California] Bee Sunday,
    June 10:1-B.

(_____)
    1966   Sunny Skies For Successful '66 Basque Festival, Elko [Nevada] Daily
    Free Press July 5:1,2.

(_____)
    1937   Suscripcion Pro-Huerfanitos Vascos [Boise] Idaho Daily Statesman May 2.

TACKE, Ray A.
    1952   Tells History of Basque People in Jordan Valley, Argus-Observer
    [Ontario, Oregon] May 12, June 12, third part (date?).

TAYLOR, Dabney
    1948   Western Basques - People of an Ancient Race, The Spokesman Review
    [Boise, Idaho] Sunday, October 17:8-9.

TAYLOR, Ron
    1968   The Basque--His Sheep A Solace for Lost Love, The Fresno [California]
    Bee Sunday, April 14:1-B.

(_____)
1967   Television Film for Basque Fest, Elko [Nevada] Daily Free Press
June 24:1.

(_____)
1966   Third Annual Basque Festival Nearing; Features New Trophy, Elko
[Nevada] Daily Free Press June 27:1.

(_____)
1966   13 Young Basque Lovlies Vie For Title of Festival Queen, Elko
[Nevada] Daily Free Press June 28:6.

(_____)
1967   Thousand Attend Annual Basque Festival, Berry Creek Barbecue, Governor
Laxalt Honored Guest, Ely [Nevada] Daily Times July 24:1.

(_____)
1937   To Acquaint Mrs. F. D. Roosevelt with relief needs, New York Times
June 15:5.

(_____)
1939   To Attend Sheepherder's Ball, Boise [Idaho] Capital News December 19.

(_____)
1967   Tonopah Basque Days Are Planned, Tonopah [Nevada] Times-Bonanza July
14:1.

(_____)
1966   US Basques Called Injustice Victims, Central California Register
June 16:1.

(_____)
1954   U.S. (gen.): House committee backs bill to admit 385 Basque sheepherders under special visas; background discussed; Senator Lehman comments,
New York Times August 6:4.

(_____)
1967   USIA Plans Basque Fest Filming, Elko [Nevada] Daily Free Press June
28:1.

(_____)
1968   U of N Receives Basque Library [Reno] Nevada State Journal March
12:10.

URZAIZ, Jaime de (Information Counselor, Embassy of Spain)
1967   The Guernica 'Myth,' in Letters to the Editor, The Washington [D.C.]
Post May 1.

(_____)
1966   Weekend of Fun, Food, Games, Opens, Elko [Nevada] Daily Free Press
July 2:1.

(_____)
1965   White Pine Basques Mark 6th Festival This Weekend, Ely [Nevada] Daily
Times July 23:1.

Unpublished Sources

BECAAS, Anita M.
   1929   The Spanish element in Nevada. Unpublished Master's thesis, Reno, University of Nevada, Department of History.

BLAUD, Henry Camille
   1957   The Basques. Unpublished Master's thesis, Stockton, California, College of the Pacific, Department of History.

CORNELL, Joseph Richard
   1959   The Acculturation of the Basque Ethnic Community in Southwestern Idaho. Unpublished Senior Essay, Indiana, University of Notre Dame, Department of Sociology.

DAVIS, Margaret
   1966   The Basque People in the United States. Ms.

DODDS, Dar
   n.d.   Song of the Basque. Ms.

DOUGLASS, William
   1967   Choice Making in Two Spanish Basque Villages. Unpublished doctoral dissertation, Chicago, University of Chicago, Department of Anthropology.

EDELFSEN, John B.
   1948   A Sociological Study of the Basques of Southwest Idaho. Unpublished doctoral dissertation, Washington State College of Washington.

GAISER, Joseph Harold
   1944   The Basques of the Jordan Valley Area. A Study in Social Process and Social Change. Unpublished doctoral dissertation, Los Angeles, University of Southern California, Department of Sociology.

GOLDARACENA, O.[rel] M.
   1893   A May ramble in Calaveras and Toulomne counties. Ms.

GÓMEZ-IBÁÑEZ, Daniel A.
   1967   The Rise and Decline of transhumance in the United States. Unpublished Master's thesis, Madison, University of Wisconsin, Department of Geography.

GRAY, Margery P.
   1955   A Population and Family Study of Basques Living in Shoshone and Boise, Idaho. Unpublished doctoral dissertation, Eugene, University of Oregon, Department of Biology.

HUGHELL, Wilma
   1939   The Community of Boise - A Study of its Educational Resources. Unpublished Master's thesis, Leland Stanford Junior University.

KELLY, James P.
   1967   The Settlement of Basques in the American West. Ms.

LOVETT, Hobart M.
    1966   Basquetry in California. Ms.

MC CULLOUGH, Sister Flavia Maria, S.H.N.
    1945   The Basques in the Northwest. Unpublished Master's thesis, Portland,
    Oregon, University of Portland.

MACGILLIVRAY, Erin
    1966   The Basques. Ms.

MAXWELL, Mary Kay
    1963   The History of the Basques in Johnson County. Ms.

PAGLIARULO, Carol M. [aria]
    1948   Basques in Stockton, A Study of Assimilation. Unpublished Master's
    thesis, Stockton, California, The College of the Pacific, Department of
    Sociology.

RUIZ, Allura Nason
    1964   The Basques - Sheepmen of the West. Unpublished Master's thesis,
    Reno, University of Nevada, Department of History.

SATHER, Clifford A.
    1961   Marriage patterns among the Basques of Shoshone, Idaho. Unpublished
    senior thesis, Portland, Oregon, Reed College, Division of History and Social
    Sciences.

WASHBURN, Harriet
    1965   The Phonemes of Wyoming Basque. Ms.

WILCOX, Mary Stevenson
    1939   A Historical Study of the Basque Race With Special Reference to the
    United States. Unpublished Master's thesis, Salt Lake City, University of Utah,
    Department of History.

Miscellaneous

(_____)
    1966   Aberri-Eguna. 1966 New York. New York, Centro Vasco-Americano.

(_____)
    1967   Aberri-Eguna. 1966 New York. New York, Centro Vasco-Americano.

ANDERSON, Bob (Producer)
    1965   The lonely Basque. Television documentary by DRON television. San
    Francisco.

ANDUIZA, John F.
    1931   Proteccion fraternal de la Fraternidad Vasca. Boise, Idaho, by the
    author.

BISCAILUZ, M. V., ed.
    Ab. 1885 Escualdun Gazeta [A Basque newspaper]. Los Angeles, California.

(_____)
1943-4   Bulletin of the Basque Delegation in the United States. New York,
Basque Government in Exile.

COMMERCIAL CLUB OF JORDAN VALLEY
n.d.   Welcome to Jordan Valley. Jordan Valley, Oregon, the Commercial Club.

(_____)
1966   Duel at the Rio Grande. A Western Company Production [film].

FESTIVAL COMMITTEE
1959   Highlights from the Western Basque Festival. Sparks, Nevada, The
Sparks Nugget.

GOYTINO, J. P., ed.
Ab. 1885 Californiako Euskal-Herria [A Basque newspaper]. Los Angeles,
California.

LARRAÑAGA, Cipriano
1967   Letter from the Delegate of the Basque Government in Exile to the
United States. New York to Basque Americans.

(_____)
1959   Thunder in the sun. Seven Arts Production. Paramount release [film].